THREE GREAT SUBSCRIPTION OFFERS
for Woodworkers

NEW!
BRITAIN'S BEST VALUE WOODWORKING MAGAZINE

NEW! ONLY £2.25 — ISSUE 10 FEBRUARY 2001

WOODWORKING

PROJECTS
Be seated
Dining room chairs
Under cover
Built-in radiator screen
Slip slide away
Kitchen draining board

TESTS
Free to breathe
DeWalt DW 790 extractor
Handy helper
The amazing Dremel
Cut to the quick
Scheppach mitre saw

Tasty tools
Biscuit jointer survey

PLUS
Hardware tests, technical advice, news, features, vital industry contacts and in-depth commentary

Make a traditional yo-yo

Furniture-making competition 2000! Your chance to enter

FURNITURE &CABINET MAKING

JUNE 2000, NO.41 £2.95

French connection
Le Ravageur factory visit

PROJECTS
■ Linen cupboard
■ Dining chairs
■ Coffee table

ON TEST
Woodcut spindle moulder ■
Record drill stand ■
Makita cordless saw ■

Accuset stapler & compressor
Kits to be won!

SAVE UP TO 20%

For makers of all types of furniture
Develop your furniture making skills

F&C breaks the mould of woodworking magazines, featuring great projects from real makers, and techniques from the experts to help you make even better furniture. Be the first to get inside information on all the latest furniture-makers' equipment, and the classic tools we all love — every month.

FOR THOSE CLOSE TO THE CUTTING EDGE!

Woodworking is a down-to-earth, practical magazine for those who love working with wood.
Packed with technical tips, product tests, advice on timber and at least three projects in every issue, it will inform and inspire all those who enjoy the practical and recreational side of woodworking.

May 2000. No.25 £2.95

Router
ROUTING IDEAS & PROJECTS FOR THE WOODWORKER

PRECISION HIGHWAY
Dovetail jigs revisited

TOOLS ON TEST
Planer/Thicknessers
WoodRat vs LittleRat
Incra's Twin Linear

PROJECTS
Oak bookcase
Bath panels
Tool chest

WIN
DeWALT EQUIPMENT WORTH £1500

SAVE UP TO 20%

Get the most from your router
The world's most versatile power tool

Whether you are a beginner or an expert you just can't afford to miss *The Router!* Get the inside story on all the latest routers and accessories — plus information, projects, techniques and advice, and tips to save money by making your own jigs and templates.

			UK £	US $	Overseas £
FURNITURE &CABINET MAKING	One year (12 issues)	Full price **10% discount**	35.40 **31.85**	73.46 **66.10**	44.25 **39.80**
	Two years (24 issues)	Full price **20% discount**	70.80 **56.60**	146.91 **117.50**	88.50 **70.80**
The Router	One year (12 issues)	Full price **10% discount**	35.40 **31.85**	73.45 **66.10**	44.25 **39.80**
	Two years (24 issues)	Full price **20% discount**	70.80 **56.60**	146.91 **117.50**	88.50 **70.80**
WOODWORKING	One year (12 issues)	Best value price	**27.00**	**50.65**	**33.75**
	Two years (24 issues)	Best value price	**54.00**	**101.25**	**67.50**

Prices shown are correct at February 2001, but may be subject to change

I would like to subscribe to.. magazine

for .... year/s

I enclose a cheque to the total value of
made payable to **GMC Publications Ltd.**   £/$
OR Please debit my credit card* to the value of   £/$

VISA ☐   AMERICAN EXPRESS ☐   ☐   MasterCard ☐   ☐ *please indicate

Account No.

Switch issue   Expiry Date

Signature .... Date ....

Mr/Mrs/Ms ....

Address ....

Postcode .... Tel ....

E-mail ....

I wish to start my subscription with the month/issue

(please complete) ....

Guild of Master Craftsman Publications will ensure that you are kept up to date on other products which will be of interest to you. If you would prefer not to be informed of future offers, please tick the box provided. ☐

CREDIT CARD HOTLINE 01273 488005
FAX: 01273 478606 EMAIL: pubs@thegmcgroup.com
or post your order to: GMC Publications Ltd
166 High Street, Lewes, East Sussex BN7 1XU England

FURNITURE &CABINET MAKING

EVERY ISSUE BRINGS YOU

- Latest developments from around the world
- Technical articles to improve your skills
- Projects for beginners and experts
- Equipment test reports
- Furniture restoration
- History of furniture making
- And much, much more...

The Router

EVERY ISSUE BRINGS YOU

- Routing news from around the world
- Technical articles to improve your skills
- Test reports to help select the right tools and equipment
- Projects for beginners and experts
- And much, much more...

WOODWORKING

EVERY ISSUE BRINGS YOU

- At least three clearly illustrated projects
- Advice on timber types and usage
- Technical tips from top industry experts
- Product tests and tool surveys
- News and diary dates
- Vital classified section

KEVIN LEY'S
FURNITURE PROJECTS

PRACTICAL DESIGNS FOR MODERN LIVING

KEVIN LEY'S
FURNITURE PROJECTS

PRACTICAL DESIGNS FOR MODERN LIVING

GUILD OF MASTER CRAFTSMAN PUBLICATIONS LTD

This collection first published 2000 by
Guild of Master Craftsman Publications Ltd,
Castle Place, 166 High Street Lewes, East Sussex BN7 1XU

ISBN 1 86108 185 5
Reprinted 2001

A catalogue record of this book is available from the British Library

Front cover photograph by Chris Skarbon

Back cover photographs and article photography by Kevin Ley, with the exception
of photograph for 'Apothecary's Chest' by Stephen Hepworth

Printed and bound by Kyodo Printing (Singapore) under the supervision of
MRM Graphics, Winslow, Buckinghamshire, UK

CONTENTS

NOTE

Every effort has been made to ensure that the information in this book is accurate at the time of writing but inevitably prices, specifications, and availability of tools will change from time to time. Readers are therefore urged to contact manufacturers or suppliers for up-to-date information before ordering tools.

MEASUREMENTS

Throughout the book instances may be found where a metric measurement has fractionally varying imperial equivalents, usually within $\frac{1}{16}$in either way. This is because in each particular case the closest imperial equivalent has been given. A mixture of metric and imperial measurements should NEVER be used – always use either one or the other.

See also detailed metric/imperial conversion charts on page 115.

INTRODUCTION

I have always enjoyed making things. Although I didn't get any training in practical subjects at school, I later fulfilled my creative urges by buying a derelict Yorkshire farmhouse and, with a couple of DIY books and some help from my brothers, completely refurbished it. Once the renovations were complete, there was time to sit down and relax – but alas, there was nothing to sit *on*! Thus began my furniture-making career, and my love affair with wood.

Pine furniture was fashionable at the time. I had a source of reclaimed pine in the form of unwanted, large packing crates, and access to recreational woodwork clubs on the RAF bases on which I served. I was thus able to learn a lot from trial and error, without too much expense – just time and many mistakes! Near one of the bases was a small timberyard specialising in native timbers, which offered me the opportunity to experiment with hardwoods – mainly elm and beech – plentiful and cheap at that time. Friends and relatives began to comment on my woodworking efforts. One or two, usually late at night (and deeply into the amber nectar) ordered pieces from me.

In the '80s, I had an option to retire early and decided on a change of direction. Perhaps naively, I decided to set up as a woodworker. I did a couple of weekend courses to improve my skills, and spent a very enjoyable four-week attachment to Rob Ellwood's workshop in Micklethwaite. I soaked up furniture designs wherever I saw them; often more interested in the pieces used to furnish the sets of films and plays than the plot. I really enjoyed working out *how* to make things, stretching my abilities, to get a result. A couple of books, Ernest Joyce's *The Technique Of Furniture-making* and *Cabinetmaking: The Professional Approach* by Alan Peters, figured high in my bedtime reading.

Making the business successful was hard work, but worth it. I soon realised that a range of skills, other than woodworking, was required. Primarily, I learned that the hand that does the books runs the business. Not least, I learned to listen to my clients, to provide what they– not I – wanted. I also found out a lot about publicity; more business came from a free display in the window of a local building society than from pictures of my furniture in glossy magazines. A news item on local TV featuring a French walnut bureau with twelve secret compartments, netted two farmers trying to sell me fallen trees!

An important spin-off of the publicity was an article about me in an early edition of *Furniture & Cabinetmaking* magazine. The editor, Paul Richardson, asked me to write something about making one of my pieces. I resisted, but was persuaded by his silver tongue – and I now write regularly for *The Router* and *Woodworking* in addition to *Furniture & Cabinetmaking*. In fact, writing about the process of making something often helps to improve my methodology, enabling me to learn from my mistakes and to pass on the improved version!

But the most important feature of my work is the wood, I love it for its own sake. I hate wasting it, using any design which detracts from its character, or finish which hides its natural beauty. As a result, I have become interested in, and influenced by, the Shaker and Arts and Crafts movements, and strive for the simplicity, elegance and quality of their designs. I have also developed a real passion for beautiful native British timbers and enjoy the almost limitless range of their properties and applications. To the makers who read this book I hope the projects that follow stimulate their own ideas, encourage them to follow their passion for wood, and really to understand its nature.

Be confident, try something a bit different – but don't frighten the horses!

Part One
PRACTICALITIES

Moving experience

How to get a step nearer to furniture-maker's heaven with a new workshop

GET A DIVORCE, leave your job, even change your bank, but don't move your workshop.

Of course I can only offer this advice after the event, and few people learn from the mistakes of others...

Having decided to move house, and finding another with a potentially much nicer workshop, I set about the project with a star in my eye. I even managed to persuade senior management that the first priority was to establish the new workshop properly before starting on the house improvements and new furniture.

"Saying goodbye to all those off-cuts which had been kept just in case"

Packing up

Packing up was full of emotion – saying goodbye to all those off-cuts which had been kept just in case...the awful piles of ageing dust, dirt and encrusted cobwebs...the happy reunions with long-lost small tools.

Cradles had to be constructed to enable cast-iron machines to be manoeuvred up the stairs to my new first floor workshop – in all several weeks of hard labour, with time to focus on the improvements to be incorporated at the new location.

I had been in the old workshop – a modern double garage, warm and dry but lacking adequate natural light – for ten years. Of course it wasn't big enough, but no workshop ever is.

I started my business there and the layout 'growed like Topsy' with me, and was due for a face lift.

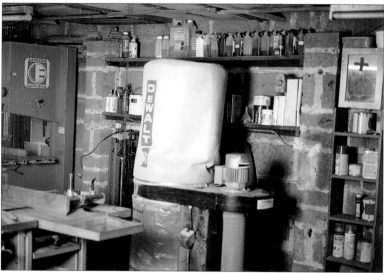

ABOVE LEFT: Right, said Fred... planer in cradle – not to be carried by its tables!

LEFT: Out with the old – after ten years, Kevin Ley is leaving all this

I wanted a nicer, safer, healthier, more efficient working environment, with more light, heat, ventilation, storage and working area and less dust, moisture and clutter, with pleasing decoration and proper fire, security, health and medical precautions.

Not much to ask.

Lighting

The new workshop is the upper floor of a modern, two storey 20ft by 20ft double garage. It is of block construction with a sound floor supported by an RSJ, and a good sized window at each end. Power and water were connected.

TOP: Splendid new workshop, outside...

RIGHT: ... and in. How long will it look like this?

The ceiling annoyingly slopes into the room, but a small loft is usable.

The windows provide good natural light and ventilation but good artificial light is also a must, so I installed a mix of general fluorescent tube lighting – with daylight tubes – and dedicated spot lights for specific areas.

I prefer a number of adjustable spot lights, fixed in the correct place, to portable lights moved around as required. They are safer and leave the bench and power points clear. Of course portable spots are still required occasionally.

Insulation

The solid walls needed insulation and a vapour barrier. British Gypsum's technical department told me about a plasterboard which has insulation bonded to its back and an integral vapour barrier, which can be glued directly on to the existing wall with a special adhesive.

I discussed costs and insulation values with my builder's merchant.

Clear installation and finishing instructions are available and it was very simple to fit and finish the board to a high standard, providing heat, sound and moisture insulation plus a smooth finish all in one go – well worth it.

The ceiling was also insulated with rolls of 100mm fibreglass.

These forms of insulation are particularly good in intermittently-heated buildings, and for controlling condensation, because they are on the inside of the wall, closest to the heat source.

Draught-proofing was also installed.

> "Triggering either alarm sets off both to give warning of impending doom at that location"

Dehumidifier, heat

I installed an Ebac domestic model dehumidifier to keep conditions suitable for working in solid wood. I don't use it during the day when I am in and out and the air is changing, but I do find that it makes a useful difference if left on while the workshop is closed down overnight and at – some – weekends.

For heat I like to burn workshop waste; this is cheap and environmentally friendly provided a clean-burn system is used, but it must be done safely in a properly designed, efficient stove.

SAFETY AND SECURITY

I tried to imagine all the things which could happen – fire, electric shock, minor and major injury, break-in and so on, deciding what I would need to do, and what I would need to do it with in order to deal with the situation. Then I thought of what I could have done to prevent it happening in the first place!

Some areas I covered were:

Fire – precautions, extinguishers, alarms
Electrical – cut-off switches, notices, correct fusing, first aid and immediate action training for shock
Medical – first aid training, medical kit, immediate action required in case of serious injury
Security – locks and alarms
Dust – dust explosions in workshops are not unknown.

My wife was – willingly – included in all the training and planning, as she is most likely to be first on the scene if I am incapacitated.
I took advice from relevant experts, added a bit of common sense, made my plans and installed the necessary equipment.

roofing felt with strong tape, available from builder's merchants, to vapour-seal and draught-proof it.

The floor was boarded over and racks made to store the wood. Sealing the wood store in this way means the dehumidifier can be used to keep the wood conditioned ready for use.

Again, I installed a small Ebac dehumidifier which is run for intermittent periods when the wood store is closed up for some time.

Dust and air

I was determined to do all I could to reduce workshop dust. The technical department at Axminster Power Tools designed a dust extraction system to meet my requirements, based around their WV 2000 vacuum dust extractor which I was able to mount downstairs in the garage.

This type of dust extractor filters the fine dust out as well as collecting the chips and shavings.

It was connected to the static machines upstairs by an under-floor ducting system, mainly comprising standard 4in rigid plastic soil pipe. The system can be reduced down to small diameter hose for use on sanders, routers and the like.

By using the extractor points and blast gates for the fixed machines, along with a small portable hose and nozzle, I can even vacuum the floor with it.

The Relax stove is designed for the job, with all accessories available, and produces a phenomenal heat output.

The suppliers at The Hot Spot gave me a great deal of useful advice concerning size of stove required and flue arrangements, siting and precautions.

Good housekeeping, care, and common-sense should be applied to the siting and use of such a stove, and, of course, fire precautions, extinguishers and alarms are essential.

The house and workshop alarm system includes a workshop heat detector and a DIY-type of ionising smoke alarm; this tends to be less affected by dust than the optical type. One alarm head is linked in the workshop and another in the house.

Triggering either sets off both to give warning of impending doom at that location. They are available at electrical suppliers, for about £10 per alarm head.

Wood store

I converted the small loft over the workshop into a wood store by sealing the overlaps of the inside

"If only someone would combine this air filter with a dehumidifier at a sensible price..."

ABOVE: A heating solution that not only keeps the workshop warm, it keeps it tidy

ABOVE RIGHT: Roof space timber store and conditioning room

BELOW: Microclene air filter mops up ambient dust

All the various connections and fittings required to tailor-make a system are available from APTC, whose technical department are extremely helpful with design and advice.

The system works very well, providing a noticeable difference in environment.

The noise level from the WV 2000 extractor is quite high, so siting it out of the workshop is a great advantage. The downside is that in winter it will suck out my precious warmth, so I may duct the filtered warm air back into the workshop in due course.

I installed a Microclene air filter to complement the extractor by filtering, cleaning and recirculating the ambient air. Because of its noise, it is used specifically to clean the air of dust not extracted by the main system – by hand-sanding and routing for instance.

It accomplishes this effectively in about 20 minutes – if only someone would combine this air filter with a dehumidifier at a sensible price...

Local advertising

Now that I am in my new area I have to set up the local business again. That involves letting people know I am here and what I do – after I have fitted the new security locks!

I will employ my tried and tested methods of local press, local shop windows, exhibitions and glossy national mags.

One idea came through my letter box as I was writing this article – a Pits business card with a photo of my work on one side and message and address on the other. They are produced at less than half the price I paid for my last set of ordinary printed business cards, and they are currently offering a further discount.

I was very impressed with their excellent offers and they seem very accessible to the idea of offering discounts, so it is always worth asking their advice on the matter.

I put a lot of work into this new workshop, trying to learn from my experience in the last one. It won't be perfect I'm sure, but it will be better, and I'm happy that it is a lot healthier. ■

SUPPLIERS

Axminster Power Tools, tel 01297 33656
Microlene Air Filters, tel 02392 502999
The Hot Spot Stoves, tel 01889 562953
Ebac, tel 01388 602602
Pits Cards, tel 01934 603600

Assessing and dealing with movement in wood, starting with drying

Coping with stress

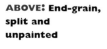

WOOD IS not inert — it moves! This fact should be uppermost when designing or making anything in wood.

I do not intend to go into great technical detail concerning the physiological reasons for such movement, but rather to concentrate on the practical steps to take to avoid furniture-making disasters.

I am assuming that the timber purchased has been air- and kiln-dried, and that the finished piece is intended for use in a centrally heated house.

The movement I am addressing here is not that caused by bad making or unsuitable design, but by the inherent nature of the wood itself.

It's of two types — movement caused by the release of stresses in the fibres by machining and dimensioning, and that caused by changes in moisture content.

Air-drying

Timber in the round may contain half its weight in water, so the felled tree must first be cut into boards and left to dry out.

Once cut to thickness the boards are separated by sticks about 25mm (1in) thick which are stacked outside to dry.

The ends are painted or have a stick nailed to them to slow down the more rapid loss from the end-grain, so reducing splitting or checking.

During the drying the stresses released by cutting the fibres of

wood, and those caused by the drying process itself, balance out. This takes about one year per inch thickness of the board.

The wood can then be said to be seasoned, air-dried and suitable for outside use. Very little general shrinkage takes place during air-drying.

Kiln-drying

The timber must now be dried further for inside use. It is placed in a sealed cabinet or kiln, and the humidity level artificially reduced to the required level. The wood loses more water until it is suitable for internal cabinet work.

The majority of the shrinkage occurs during this process.

I have given no figures, percentages of water by weight

or relative humidity levels because these are difficult, expensive to measure and not constant.

Air-drying is to the average humidity level in that place at that time. Kiln-drying depends on the operator, and the level to which the wood is taken.

How long the wood has been out of the kiln, how it was stored before purchase, and how it is treated afterwards can also have a significant effect on the moisture content.

ABOVE: End-grain, split and unpainted

LEFT: End-grain, split and nailed

> "Don't keep it in a damp garage with wet cars coming in and out, or even a dedicated timber store if it is not heated and damp-proofed"

ABOVE: **Quarter-sawn oak end-grain table top —** *right*

ABOVE: **End-grain, painted**

Buying timber

A reputable timber merchant with whom a good relationship can be established is worth his weight in gold. Explain your requirements, ask when it was cut and how long it was air-dried, to what level it was kilned, and buy the best quality material you can afford.

Observe the storage conditions, feel the weight and touch the surface.

I long ago realised that the selection, felling, conversion, drying and storage of timber is a very highly skilled task, one that is best left to experts. What I want to do is make furniture well out of materials I can trust. It is important, however, to take responsibility for the material when it comes into the maker's care, to understand the principles and apply them, and to put the final touches to the process.

Storing timber

Once timber leaves the kiln it starts to adjust its moisture content to its surroundings, so it must be stored in conditions as close as possible to those in which it is to live as a piece of furniture.

Don't keep it in a damp garage with wet cars coming in and out, or even a dedicated timber store if it is not heated and damp-proofed.

Keep stocks of timber in the warmest, driest conditions possible — in my case the area between the beams in my insulated workshop roof.

If the storage temperature and moisture conditions are close to those of the end use, the timber can be stored and conditioned with sticks between the boards, allowing free air flow.

Make sure the sticks are lined up directly over each other so that the weight is borne through the sticks and the boards are not deformed.

Sheets of newspaper can be placed between the boards instead to suck some of the moisture out.

If the storage conditions are not as dry as the end use conditions store the boards flat on top of each other, with no air gap, and cover with a waterproof sheet to minimise the moisture intake.

Moisture movement

The main movement takes place not in the length but across the grain. Movement per inch along the circumference of the growth ring is about twice that per inch between the growth rings.

From this understanding it should be apparent why quarter-or radially-sawn wood is more stable than tangentially sawn, *see diagrams.*

The key to understanding moisture-related movement in wood is in being aware that the major amount of movement occurs when the moisture content is reduced from air-dried to a level suitable for interior furniture use and vice versa.

Wood will always move if its moisture content changes, and it will always try to equalise its moisture content to its surrounding environment, absorbing moisture from damp air and losing it to dry air.

As it absorbs moisture it will swell and as it loses moisture it will shrink — no matter how old the wood.

The level of moisture in the air

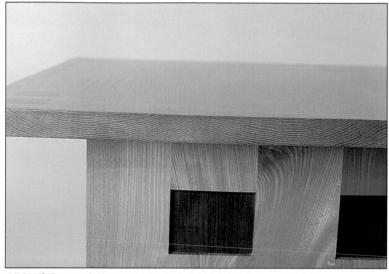

ABOVE: Tangentially-sawn elm end-grain table top — *wrong*

"The desk shrank, took up all its allowance and cracked along the top. My client said that when they entered the room they had to hang out of the windows to breathe!"

RIGHT: Laburnum oysters showing growth ring circumference and spacing

ABOVE: Drawer casings in stick with a weight on top

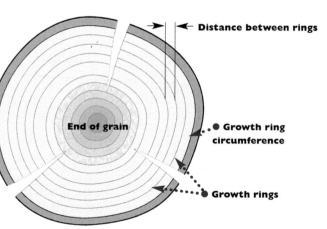

Distance between rings

End of grain

Growth ring circumference

Growth rings

varies from summer to winter, warm summer air holding more water than that of cold winter. When this winter air is brought inside and centrally heated it can hold more water, which it takes out of its surroundings.

Drying effect

This is the drying effect which causes shrinkage in wood. The change of moisture content in the air — relative humidity — together with temperature and weather conditions, causes most solid wood furniture in a centrally heated environment to be in a constant state of movement from summer to winter.

It tends to swell in summer and shrink in winter, but fortunately wood reacts slowly to changes of

humidity so the movement is gradual.

Moisture content change varies according to the variety of timber. I usually allow for about 3mm (^{1}/$_8$in) movement per 300mm (12in) of width of board across the grain direction in normal conditions, but adjustments must be made in the light of experience, and the end use conditions.

It follows, then, that establishing the likely conditions in which the piece will end up is important when judging the allowance for movement.

A desk I made recently in best quality, kiln-dried, quarter-sawn oak (*Quercus robur*) was left in a room unoccupied for some weeks in mid winter, with the radiators left inadvertently at full

chat with no thermostats!

The desk shrank, took up all its allowance and cracked a full 3mm (^{1}/$_8$in) along the top. My client said that when they entered the room they had to hang out of the windows to breathe!

Fortunately he accepted responsibility and a repair was made to everyone's satisfaction.

After six weeks near a radiator in Bowes Museum the drawers of the Apothecary's Chest in burr elm (*Ulmus procera*), simply

ABOVE: Movement is twice as much per inch along circumference as between growth rings; more shrinkage on the long outside rings causes checks and cracks

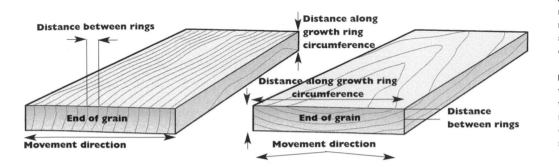

Distance between rings

Distance along growth ring circumference

Distance along growth ring circumference

End of grain

Movement direction

End of grain

Distance between rings

Movement direction

FAR LEFT: Small amount of growth ring circumference included, movement fairly even and at right-angles to the faces, minimising distortion

LEFT: Little movement in the thickness of the board — between the growth rings — but a lot of movement along the circumference, causing the board not only to shrink but to distort or 'cup'

wouldn't open. I was puzzled until I discovered that the museum has humidifiers to protect all the artefacts that don't like central heating, and the wood had swollen, not shrunk as I had expected.

A few days in my warm, dry workshop with the drawers out to allow good air circulation, and some small adjustments, rectified the problem and it is now ready to live in a house again.

Secondary machining

Wood is constructed of fibres all pulling in slightly different directions but balancing each other out. When the wood is sawn or planed some of the fibres are cut, releasing the pull they were exerting, and allowing the remaining fibres to pull the wood into another shape.

The release of stresses is usually a relatively short-term effect in seasoned timber, and once complete should stabilise. If the wood is clamped in position, some of the stresses will be taken out by stretching the remaining fibres, thus minimising the distortion.

Properly seasoned, kiln-dried timber is stable on starting a job, but dimensioning it on the planer or saw cuts other fibres, releasing other tensions.

To minimise the resultant distortion, cut the pieces oversize and leave to settle overnight — or longer — on stickers, under a weight, in a warm dry place.

Finish to size and again store the pieces on stickers with a weight on the top until needed.

Workshop conditions

A warm dry workshop is a prerequisite to serious cabinetmaking.

Look at the basic construction — aesthetics count for nothing if it is damp, or can't be heated. ■

72"

30"

•••● Dehumidifier

ABOVE: Home-conditioning cabinet or kiln

HOME-KILNING

A KILN OR conditioning cabinet for home use for small amounts of timber can be made easily. Its box construction uses a home dehumidifier to remove the water from the air and from wood stacked inside.

Make the box as air-tight as possible and line it with polythene to prevent fresh damp air entering, or moisture permeating the walls.

The dehumidifier should be set to the manufacturer's recommended level for domestic interiors, and the water it removes from the inside air piped to the outside.

The wood should be stacked as for air-drying, with plenty of room to allow the air to circulate.

The wood must be air-dried and seasoned first to allow as much water as possible to be removed, the machining stresses to stabilise and the distribution of water in the wood to even out.

This secondary drying process in the home-made kiln should be gentle, with plenty of time allowed.

Assume thoroughly air-dried wood has a water content of 20% by weight. Weigh a test piece and mark its weight on it. After about a month in the 'kiln', re-weigh the test piece; when it has lost about 8% of its original weight it is about ready.

I would recommend that the dehumidifier is not left on all the time, but is switched off every fourth day or so to allow the water in the wood to distribute itself evenly.

I use it very successfully for burr elm (*Ulmus sp*), which I find difficult to get commercially kiln-dried.

The cabinet can also be used to condition kiln-dried timber for a week or two as a precaution before making it up. Again, the timber is dimensioned slightly oversize and stacked on sticks in the cabinet for a few days.

The longer such timber has been out of the kiln, or in poor storage conditions, the more important this is.

LEFT: Photo 1
Pine blanket box
showing grain
direction around
sides

BELOW: Photo 2
Lid open, showing
braces

Turning up the heat

How to allow for movement when making pieces of furniture

A MAJOR CAUSE of dispute and disappointment in custom-made solid wood furniture is movement occurring after a piece is made — sometimes with disastrous results!

In the past, I have looked at how and why wood moves and how to minimise that movement in timber selected for cabinetmaking. Now I will turn my attention to making allowances for the movement which will inevitably take place when the furniture is made.

The suitability and characteristics of solid wood furniture must be discussed with clients, who must have its limitations explained so as to prevent blatant mistreatment —

like standing the piece in front of a radiator or in a conservatory in full sun!

With the advent of stable sheet materials people tend to forget — or perhaps have never learned — how to look after solid wood.

Shrinkage cracks which may verify antiques — and even increase their value — will not be accepted in modern solid wood furniture. Part of a modern designer-maker's skill and responsibility is to allow for central heating.

Principles

In spite of all precautions taken to select, store, and condition wood properly it will still move as its moisture content changes to match that of the surrounding air.

This movement is an irresistible force; it cannot be prevented or restrained, and must be allowed for in the making. In a normally heated domestic environment wood will tend to expand across the grain — not along it — in the summer, and shrink in the winter.

This means that while the length of a board will not change, the width and, to a smaller extent, the thickness will. The problem really is that simple — it's finding the solutions which can give the headaches!

Grain direction

I have chosen a simple pine blanket box, *see photo 1*, with which to illustrate a number of methods to negate the effects of movement.

> **"Clients must have limitations explained so as to prevent blatant mistreatment — like standing the piece in front of a radiator or in a conservatory in full sun!"**

Firstly all four sides should have the grain running the same way, around the box. As the potential movement will be across the width of the grain, the only effect of shrinkage will be a slight difference in the height of the box which will probably go unnoticed.

Dovetailing the joints to prevent any bowing or cupping will ensure this part of the carcass is sound and stable.

It can also be seen from this photograph that the boards used in the top, chosen deliberately for their nice figure, are tangentially sawn and so liable to cupping.

Timber tends to have a different moisture content on the outside faces than core due to its greater exposure to the surrounding air's moisture content, so while thicknessing these pieces I would be careful to take the same amount off each face to keep the balance even and reduce the tendency to cup. I would also leave them to stabilise for some time in stick under a weight.

Clearance holes

Braces fitted under the top will help keep it flat, *see photo 2*. The grain in the braces is, however, running across the width of the top boards, so that although the top will expand and contract across its width, the length of the braces will remain unchanged.

To prevent the top from cracking or buckling, the braces are screwed to the top through double-countersunk holes. These give clearance to allow the screw to move from side to side with the top movement, while still

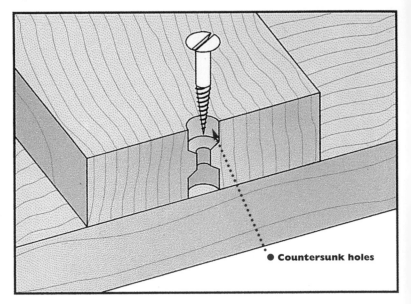

● Countersunk holes

ABOVE: Fig I Double countersunk hole for screw and brace

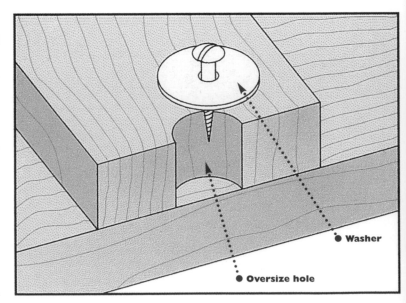

● Washer

● Oversize hole

ABOVE: Fig 2 Oversize hole for screw with washer

ABOVE: Photo 4 Frame and panel door

"Frames with the grain running across carcass sides, for instance those accommodating drawers, must allow for side movement without distorting the frame or the side"

RUNNING FREE

THE ABILITY of the runner to enable free movement of the drawer is an important feature of solid carcass construction. The ends of the front and back rails are glued into the sides, but the side rails are fitted dry into locating housings in the carcass sides, so allowing the sides to expand and contract by means of the expansion gap, *see fig 5*.

Colin Eden-Eadon adds: One other way of accommodating carcass movement for drawer runners is to construct solid dividers, always ensuring that the grain direction follows that of the rest of the carcass work. An alternative, less expensive timber may be used, the front edge being lipped to match the finish timber of the piece.

ABOVE: Photo 5 Drawer frame showing expansion gap

holding it flat, *see fig 1*. Of course the braces must not be glued to the top.

The holes are plugged with matching pine to improve the appearance. A suitably oversize hole, or a slot, could also be used with a round-headed screw and washer if movement is likely to be considerable, *see figs 2 and 3*, but this method is unsightly.

Fixed panel

Problems would ensue if the base of the box was of the same construction as the top — and needless to say it isn't. The underneath, *see photo 3*, reveals a frame and panel. With no movement in the sides relative to the base, the latter shouldn't move either.

The frame is arranged in such a way that the grain runs virtually in the same direction as the sides. The centre panel is ply and, as it will not move, it is glued in all round for added stability. The base can be glued, screwed and plugged directly to the sides.

Floating panel

Photo 4 is of a framed and fielded panelled door. The grain runs through the length of the frame components so it will move very little in its perimeter dimensions, retaining its fit in the carcass. The panel is not glued but fitted in a groove in the frame, allowing free shrinkage across its width without adverse effects.

If required, the panel can be spot glued at its top and bottom centres to locate it in the frame and ensure equal movement on each side, *see fig 4*.

Drawer frame

Frames with their grain running across carcass sides, for instance drawer runners, must allow side-to-side movement of the carcass to avoid distortion. This can be achieved by leaving the rear mortices and tenons of the frame dry, and allowing an expansion gap, *see panel and photo 5*. If the sides of the frame are then fixed only at the front of the carcass,

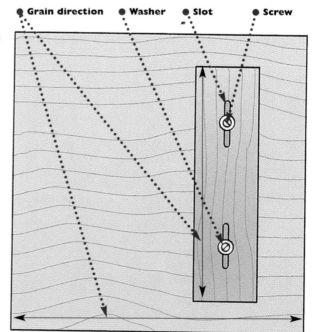

● **Grain direction**   ● **Washer**   ● **Slot**   ● **Screw**

ABOVE: Fig 3 Screw and washer in slot

Sealing its surfaces can slow down the movement of moisture in and out of wood, but completely sealing all the surfaces without total immersion of the finished piece is difficult, so it will eventually stabilise to the average moisture level in its immediate environment.

I have had some success with oil on burr elm (*Ulmus sp*). The burr can be quite porous; because of its wild grain, and by keeping the first coat wet as long as possible, the oil is encouraged to penetrate deeply.

I think this fills a layer of cells under the surface, which then, instead of absorbing the moisture, becomes a barrier to moisture pick-up, helping to even out sudden peaks and troughs.

RIGHT: Fig 4
Frame and
floating panel
construction

Spot glued to
locate panel in
centre and
equalise
movement ●

Floating fielded
panel let into
groove in frame
but not glued all
round ●

Frame ●

They are fixed to the frame directly with screws through countersunk holes, and to the top through slots — again allowing the necessary movement while holding the top flat.

The two slots at are right-angles to each other — be sure to put the screw into the right one!

Precautions

A number of precautions should be taken to minimise movement in the timber used in the making of furniture. While clients must also be told what constitutes suitable conditions for solid wood furniture, they must also accept that the wood will move as it adjusts to its environment.

All my suggestions are based on the premise that wood moves across but not along the grain. With that in mind all sorts of ingenious solutions can be devised to solve design problems. ■

shrinkage of the carcass sides can occur without problems.

Fixed tops

Solid tops on tables must be allowed to expand and contract across their width, but be held flat to prevent any twisting or cupping.

The simplest solution is for the underside of the top to be held flat by wooden buttons which have a tongue located in a slot in the underframe. The body of the button is screwed directly to the underside of the top, allowing the top to expand and contract across its width while being held flat to the frame.

Set the slot slightly low to pull the top down as the buttons' screws are tightened up.

Photo 6 shows detail of the same top with one of the buttons removed and replaced by an expansion plate for demonstration purposes.

These plates can be used instead of the wooden buttons.

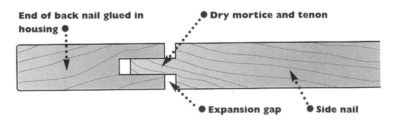

End of back nail glued in
housing ●

● Dry mortice and tenon

● Expansion gap   ● Side nail

Fig 5 Drawer frame showing gap and dry joint

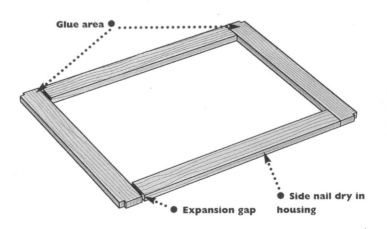

Glue area ●

● Expansion gap

● Side nail dry in
housing

Part Two
PROJECTS

Three in one

How to make a nest of tables

Nest, or stacking, occasional tables are useful in providing maximum table-top area when required, while occupying minimum floor space when not in use. They are usually of simple construction, but still require a range of basic making operations and techniques, repeated a number of times. They are useful practice pieces – that give a little more satisfaction than the ubiquitous woodwork-class stool!

Design

Many different arrangements are possible, from the Long John side table with two free-standing tables under, to a nest of up to five – four suspended under the main table, sliding in and out on bearers.

For this project the primary use was as a side table, so the dimensions of that table were the starting point.

The design specified traditional construction, with stop chamfered, rather than turned, legs.

The overhang of the tops and the thickness of the legs reduced the size of the smaller tables by considerable steps. By the time I got to the third table it would only just hold a bottle and a glass, so a fourth table was obviously not required!

Increasing the size of the top of the largest table, and/or reducing the top's overhang, and replacing the legs with thinner, solid sides, would allow larger tops and/or more under-tables.

Timber selection

The timber of choice was elm, and I had some English or common elm, *Ulmus procera*, which had been air-dried for some years. The wood was hard, and dark in colour, with a course texture and some nice figuring.

Timber preparation

As of all the elms English is the most unstable, it must be thoroughly conditioned to its end-use environment. Select what you require, and mark out the various components about 10% oversize. The pieces for the table tops are cut from the best figured boards, choosing the very best wood for the largest table, as this will be in permanent full view.

I stacked and sticked all the pieces and put them in my conditioning cabinet

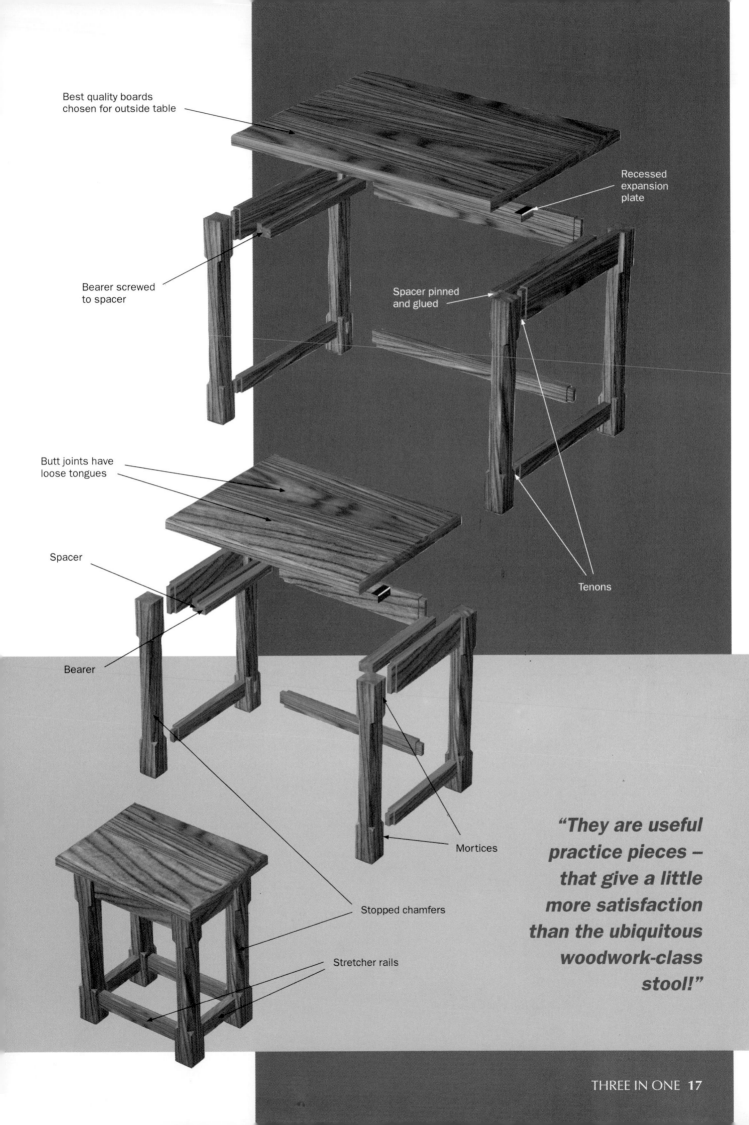

Best quality boards
chosen for outside table

Recessed
expansion
plate

Bearer screwed
to spacer

Spacer pinned
and glued

Tenons

Butt joints have
loose tongues

Spacer

Bearer

Mortices

Stopped chamfers

Stretcher rails

*"They are useful
practice pieces –
that give a little
more satisfaction
than the ubiquitous
woodwork-class
stool!"*

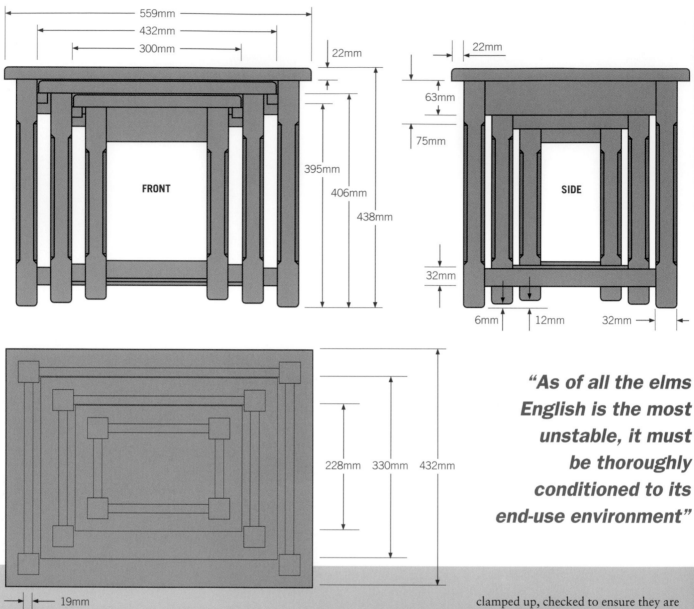

"As of all the elms English is the most unstable, it must be thoroughly conditioned to its end-use environment"

for a month. If you do not have access to a conditioning cabinet the pieces should be placed, similarly stacked and sticked, for as long as possible, in the room in which the tables will eventually live, or a similar environment.

Tops

The selected boards are faced and thicknessed, and matched for the most pleasing figure and colour, trying to ensure that the figure runs through the joins to disguise them. The grain in my elm was pretty wild, so alternating the cupping tendency of the boards was irrelevant. I am not convinced about the value of this practice anyway – I prefer to address the likely movement in one direction rather than the corrugated iron effect!

The joining edges are machine-planed on the jointer, then hand-planed to remove the machine ripples which would weaken the glue joint.

The fit of the joining edges is slightly concave, touching at each end with an approximately 1.5mm (¹⁄₁₆in) gap at the centre. This helps the clamps pull up tight, and allows for extra shrinkage at the ends, if there is any further drying out.

The joining edges are then slotted for a loose ply tongue to add strength. The boards are marked where they will be finally cut to size, and the slots stopped 25mm (1in) short of those marks so that the final trimming will not expose the tongue. Cascamite glue is applied to the slots, edges and tongues, the tops are

clamped up, checked to ensure they are flat, and left to set.

Legs

The legs are cut to length, and dimensioned to 38mm (1½in) cross section. The mortises are cut for the top frame and bottom rails – I used the morticer on my planer, although a router would also have been suitable. The floor-end of the legs is rounded over to ¼ radius to prevent splintering and aid sliding on carpets.

The stopped chamfers were cut on a router, all starting 75mm (3in) in from the ends, and finished with a sharp scraper.

Frames

The pieces for the top frames and bottom rails are dimensioned and the tenons cut to fit the mortises in the legs. These are dry-fitted to check accuracy. It

A cabinet scraper is used to clean up the stopped chamfers

Elm varieties

Elm can vary considerably in colour, texture, figure and stability depending on which of the sub-species it is. Dutch elm is not as dark and has straighter grain than English, with less figure, and is more stable. Wych elm is even straighter grained, paler in colour, often with a green streak, and the most stable of the three. Beware when buying to match previous work!

Although all three types are affected by Dutch elm disease there are still reasonable supplies of timber available, mainly from the North. It is being replanted in the South.

"It is particularly important that the joints on the bottom rails of the two larger tables are a really good fit"

Neatly stacked away, the tables won't take up much space

is particularly important that the joints on the bottom rails of the two larger tables are a really good fit. They have to be as strong as possible as there would be no front bottom rails to complete the square and brace the legs fully.

Assembly

Now the legs, top frame pieces, and bottom rails are finished and sanded down to 150 grit. First all the sides are glued up, clamped, checked for square, surplus glue removed, and left to set. The bearers are fitted on the inside of the sides of the larger two tables to carry the under tables. A 25mm by 10mm

Side rail

Recessed expansion plate

25mm

Bearer

Side spacer

Leg

BEARER DETAIL

Finish

An oiled finish was preferred for these tables but I had my doubts about its durability on the tops. They were coarse textured, with a wild grain, some of which, because of its direction, was porous. The principle of an oiled finish is not to build up a layer on top of the wood, but to soak it in to the top surface, wiping off any surplus.

I felt that there would be an unavoidable build-up of a layer of oil on this surface, and it would mark easily. The likely use for the tables would entail contact with hot and cold liquids and alcohol. I could see a constant need for re-oiling.

The compromise was to give everything one coat of Liberon finishing oil, which I find thinner and more penetrative than some other Danish oils, carefully wiping off all surplus with kitchen tissue. This coat gave the main colour change to the wood.

I had contacted the technical department of Liberon and been assured that polyurethane varnish would key to their finishing oil, provided it was a single sub coat and allowed to dry for at least 24 hours.

Thereafter all but the tops were given the usual five or six thin coats

of oil, at 24 hour intervals, wiping off all surplus, and cutting back with a Scotchbrite grey pad between coats.

The tops were given 4 thin coats of satin-finish polyurethane varnish, applied with a sponge pad, which was allowed to build up to a smooth finish. The first two coats were cut back with 320 grit on a hard sanding block to allow the grain to fill. Further coats were cut back with the grey pad to give a similar sheen to the oiled finish.

The end result was very satisfactory, the overall effect being of an oiled finish but with durable, easy to maintain tops.

The expansion plates on the smallest of the three tables

"As the smallest table will have no table below it, recesses are not necessary, and the expansion plates are fitted normally"

(1in by ⅜in) spacer is pinned and glued between the legs, flush with the inside edge, and the 19mm by 19mm (¾in by ¾in) bearer screwed through the spacer to the side, leaving 25mm (1in) clearance from the top of the bearer to the underside of the table top.

Two expansion plates are fitted to the sides of the tables, above the spacers, through which the tops will be attached.

"They work well as occasional tables and have also been used as seats, step-ups, and even missiles when people have tripped over them!"

Those on the larger two tables are fitted proud of the tops of the sides. They will be recessed into their table tops so that the plates and fixing screws will not foul the top of the sliding table below. As the smallest table will have no table below it, recesses are not necessary, and the expansion plates are fitted normally.

Next, the sides are fitted together to the top frame pieces and the bottom rails – no front top frame, or rails on the larger two tables. They are clamped, checked for square, surplus glue removed, and left to set.

The tops are now finally cut to size, and the edges rounded over to 6mm (¼in) radius. They are offered up to the assembled frames, the expansion plates positions are marked, and the tops removed. The recesses are cut in the two larger table-tops deep enough to clear the plates and screw heads, with

clearance in the recess to the front and rear of the plate to allow the top to move.

The tops are finished to 150 grit, and fixed to the frames by screws through the expansion plates, making sure to screw through the correct slot – remember the movement is across the grain!

Conclusion

These tables have been in constant use for a number of years. They work well as occasional tables and have also been used as seats, step-ups, and even missiles when people have tripped over them! All without apparent harm.

The finish has proved successful, the tops are wiped with a damp cloth and the remainder gets, infrequently, a thin coat of teak oil. Though simple to make, their very usefulness makes them a satisfying project. ■

Angles and tapers

How to make a Shaker-style chest of drawers with tapered sides

THE CLIENT had seen the burr elm apothecary's chest I had made in an exhibition in the Bowes Museum. He liked it and decided to buy it – and at the same time asked about having a small desk and chest of drawers made.

I happened to have in the house an oak, tapered pedestal desk, which I had just completed for another client. When he saw it he was very taken with the idea of the tapering pedestal, and decided to have one on his desk.

He then saw a tall Shaker-style chest I had made some time ago to my wife's specifications. He again liked it and decided, albeit nervously, that the taper should be used on this companion chest of drawers, to link the two pieces.

Timbers
My client was very keen on the burr elm, *Ulmus spp*, not only because of its beautiful figure, but because it was gathered locally from the hedgerows, where elms have all but disappeared.

We rapidly recognised the impracticability of using all burr for the piece – not least because I didn't have enough – as it would be unsuitable for most parts of the construction.

The final decision was to use burr for the drawer fronts, to maximise its impact, while still using a relatively small amount. The remainder of the carcass construction was to be in fumed, oiled Brazilian mahogany, *(Swietenia macrophylla)*, to provide a contrast of colour and figure, emphasise the burr, and give a rich final look.

The chest was to be used for clothes storage so cedar of Lebanon, *(Cedrus libani)* with its distinctive pleasant smell and insect repellent properties, was chosen for the drawer casings.

Selection
The Brazilian mahogany with its relative lack of figure, consistent grain and absence of faults was easily selected, cut and dressed oversize, stacked with separating sticks and put in my conditioning cabinet, *see Coping with stress, page 7.*

Likewise the cedar of Lebanon for the drawer casings – this stack was weighted on the top.

Selecting the burr was much more demanding. The surfaces had to be examined carefully for figure, colour and faults. Then the provisionally chosen pieces marked with chalk and put together to try and guess the overall effect. Next they were cut oversize, faced,

thicknessed, checked again, then wiped with white spirit to show an approximation of the final finished colour.

After a final examination in detail, confirmation of best face, orientation, and position, the pieces were clearly marked, stacked, sticked, weighted on top, and placed in the conditioning cabinet, where they were left for a few days.

The mahogany was removed to begin the project, but the drawer material was left in as long as was possible.

Carcass construction
The carcass construction was fairly standard with the sides housed directly into the top, and the drawer frames housed into the sides.

The complication was in the taper. To make the measurements of distances and angles easier it was essential to draw the front of the chest, full size, on to a piece of hardboard.

Then I transferred the angle of the sides from the vertical, accurately onto a suitable piece of plastic, hardboard would do, about 100mm (4in) square, cut it, and used it as a reference for all machine settings and angle cuts for this piece.

Sides
The sides were made up first, each from two widths of mahogany. The figure was matched carefully and the joint strengthened with a ply loose tongue.

A 10mm (⅜in) deep by 5mm (³⁄₁₆in) wide slot was cut in the sides and top for the back, taking care to stop the slot in the top short of the overhang.

Next the housings for the drawer frames were cut, except for the top and bottom – these housings were 19mm (¾in) wide by 10mm (⅜in) deep, at the shallowest side, to take the full thickness of the frames.

The top frame housing was 10mm (⅜in) wide and offset down to avoid the tenon for the top.

The bottom housing was also 10mm (⅜in) and offset up, to leave room for the cutout to form the side feet.

All the housings were cut at the required angle by fixing a block onto the router base to raise one side. The ends were chiselled square, and the housings cleaned out carefully.

LEFT: Tapered sides require tapered drawers

BELOW: This Shaker-style chest of drawers provided the proportions

Frames

The frames were made up from 50mm (2in) by 19mm (¾in) mahogany, the sides tenoned into mortises in the front and back rails.

The back rails were made 1mm longer than the front rails to make for easier drawer-fitting and running.

The front joint was glued, the rear joint dry fitted and an expansion gap left to allow for subsequent movement.

The shoulders of the frames were marked on the front and back with the angle marker, 10mm (⅜in) in on the bottom edge, and cut 10mm (⅜in) deep with a tenon saw.

The top and bottom frames were rebated to 10mm (⅜in), and all the frames were individually dry fitted and finished.

Feet

Housings for the front feet were cut 6mm (¼in) deep on the front of the sides and the bottom frame. The feet were cut to size, dry fitted and finished.

Cutouts for the feet on the sides were made and the edges finished.

The angled shoulders on the top of the sides, where they fit into the top, were cut at the front and back, and the sides finished.

Top

The top was made up from three widths of 19mm (¾in) mahogany; like the sides, the figure was carefully matched and the joints were strengthened with a ply loose tongue.

Care was taken to stop the slot for this tongue well short of the edge, so that it was not exposed when the edge was chamfered.

Next the angled housings in the top, to take the sides, were cut. This was done in the same way as the angled housings in the sides, which were dry fitted to the top to check for a fit.

These housings were 1mm further apart at the back to correspond with the extra length of the back of the frames.

The chamfer on the underside of the top was then marked, and a strip of wood was clamped to the top, in the relevant place, as a fence. A sharp jack plane was used to remove the bulk of the waste.

The plane was sharpened, reset to fine, and the final light finishing cut made.

A light sanding finished the job.

Back

The back was made from 5mm mahogany faced MDF. I intended to use it as a brace during the assembly and gluing up, to help keep the shape of the carcass.

It was cut accurately using the full size drawing on hardboard, finished and check-fitted.

Assembly

Assembly had to be approached with even more care than usual. The top could not be fitted after the frames because of the angled housings, so the first stage of the gluing up would be the sides, frames, and top, in one go.

I prepared everything carefully, finishing all the pieces I could, and dry-fitted the whole thing. I used battens with shallow notches cut in them to hold the sash clamps level and stop them slipping .

Cascamite was made up and applied to the front and back of the frame housings, leaving the sides of the frames a dry running fit to allow for future movement.

As the grain of the top and sides was running in the same direction, glue was applied all along the housings in the top and to the top of front and back rails of the top frame.

The back was dry-fitted to help keep the taper even. The frames and top were positioned and sash clamps were placed across the front and back.

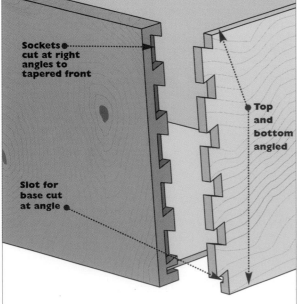

Sockets cut at right angles to tapered front

Top and bottom angled

Slot for base cut at angle

Angled base block in use cutting housings

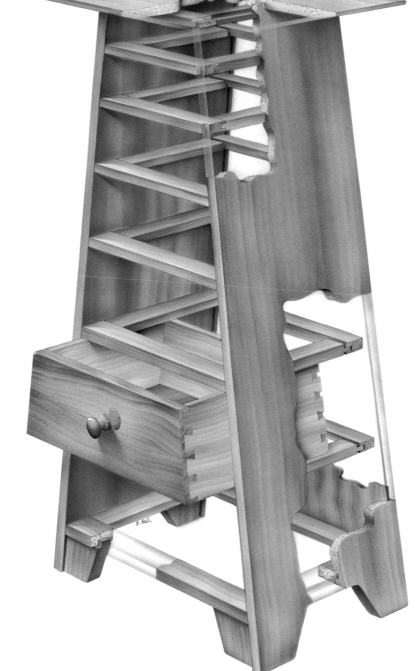

FUMING

The carcass was wiped over with white spirit to show any glue marks. It was left to dry and hand sanded to 320 grit.

It is essential to remove all surplus glue before fuming, particularly around joints. Check the whole piece for marks, blemishes, and raised grain – it will be too late afterwards!

It was then placed in a polythene tent with some saucers of about 5fl oz of 880 ammonia and left for 24 hours.

Fuming works particularly well with oak and the longer you leave it, the darker it will get. Make sure the tent is well sealed with tape. Alternatively you can make a sealed box, but this is really only practical for smaller items.

Ammonia is dangerous and toxic. Contact with skin and eyes will be extremely painful and even momentary inhalation will cause nausea and vomiting. Ammonia has a particularly adverse effect on the eyes and contact causes permanent damage.

Protective clothing must be worn, including strong anti-chemical gauntlets, a face mask suitable for coping with toxic fumes, eye protection and suitable coveralls.

Use the chemical outdoors if possible; if used indoors make sure the working area is well ventilated, adding extra fans if necessary and ensuring that the fumes are routed to a safe place.

Never flush into the drainage system, instead, put it into a container after use for proper disposal.

The evenness of the taper was checked by measuring the diagonals, which should be equal, as with a square construction.

A further check was done with the plastic angle setter on each drawer frame and all seemed to be well.

The top was held to the top rail with G-clamps and all was left overnight to set.

The next day the back was carefully slid out, glue applied to the slot and the backs of the back rails, and the back replaced and pinned to the rails. Glue was applied to the foot housings and the feet fitted.

Fitting drawer components

Now that the carcass was complete I fitted the drawer components. The top and bottom of the sides needed to be cut at an angle so I set the table saw blade and the planer fence to the correct angle using my trusty angle setter. I also cut the slots for the drawer bases on the table saw while the angle was set.

Next I cut and fitted the drawer fronts, remembering that because of the taper, anything taken off the bottom edge also reduces the width. To reduce the height without altering the width, plane the top edge.

I cut the slots in the fronts to take the drawer bases. Using the fronts as a pattern I cut the backs. The backs were 5mm (³⁄₁₆in) lower than the sides, they fitted on top of the base, and because of the taper, must be lined up in exactly the right place.

I cut strips of 5mm (³⁄₁₆in) ply by 13mm (½in)wide, and fitted it in the base slot cut in the drawer fronts.

LEFT: Another tapered carcass being cramped up showing cawls to ensure even pressure on all joints

The backs were cut to the correct height, put on the edge of the bench and the fronts offered up to them until the backs registered on to the protruding ply. They were then marked with a knife, cut and checked for fit.

After the backs had been cut I oiled the backs of the drawer fronts to help stabilise the burr, applying several coats before the drawers were assembled.

Drawer dovetails

The dovetails were marked on the sides, cut just short of the line on the bandsaw, and finished with a chisel.

The positioning of the pins was critical as they would be cut at right angles to the tapered front. Consequently the sides would move down the front as the joint was assembled.

I marked the horizontal and used a set square to measure the amount of this offset. Allowing for the offset, I marked the pins on the edges of the drawer fronts. The backs of the pins were marked with a set square from the edge of the front, and the waste removed with a router, dovetail saw, and chisel.

The joints were glued up and the drawers assembled, with the cedar of Lebanon faced MDF bases glued in all round for extra strength.

Pulls were made from offcuts of burr, and pegged, glued, and screwed into the fronts.

The drawers and stops were fitted remembering that if any adjustment to the height was made from the bases, it would result in a corresponding reduction in the width of the drawer, because of the taper.

Finish

Danish oil was the preferred finish as it brings out the deep richness of the figure

and colour of the burr – and the colour and silky finish of the mahogany. What is more, it improves with time and tender loving care.

The burr was quite porous and the oil penetrated well into the wood, helping to stabilise it.

The first coat was liberally applied, left to soak in, and refreshed every 15 to 20 minutes until no more would soak in.

The burr took considerably more oil and more coats than the less

porous mahogany. The chest was wiped off with a soft cloth between coats and no oil was allowed to build up on the surface.

It was left to harden for 24 hours in a warm dry place. The surface was then cut back with a Scotchbrite grey pad, further light coats applied every 24 hours – and cut back with the Scotchbrite pad, until the desired effect was achieved.

Conclusion

I was pleased with the unusual look of this tapered piece and, more to the point, so was my client!

I enjoyed the challenge of making the tapered carcass and the tapered drawers. The combination of burr and mahogany was effective, and husbanded my ever depleting stocks of solid burr.

When viewed from the front the majority of the chest shows burr nicely framed in fumed mahogany, getting maximum use out of the burr used. ■

BELOW: Pins are marked out at right angles to tapered drawer fronts

BELOW RIGHT: Sides are assembled moving down the tapered front allowing for the offset

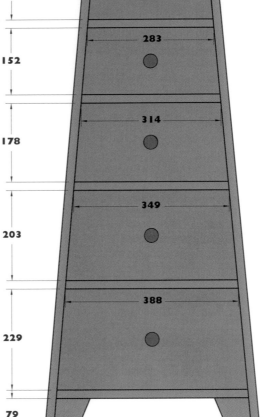

Keeping up w

Making a Shaker-style tall clock

FOR QUITE SOME TIME I have wanted to make a long case clock. Not one of those massively ornate monsters, but something elegant and simple. The obvious place to start researching my design was with Shaker furniture. In Thos Mosers' excellent book *How to Build Shaker Furniture* I found a good example which could be modified. It was a fairly standard Shaker design, with simple lines and no ornament, although it was bigger than I wanted – and was painted dark red! I will never understand how the Shakers reconciled their philosophy of simplicity with their habit of painting their furniture in, sometimes quite garish, colours.

"The obvious place to start researching my design was with Shaker furniture"

Clock

I decided to use sycamore (*Acer pseudoplatanus*) which, with its light airy look, really suits Shaker styles. I would add interest with the careful use of ripple sycamore and a fumed oak door pull.

I chose a traditional two-weight clock movement and a 'bim-bam' chime, with a simple black and white dial and plain black hands – all of which were in the Yorkshire Clock Builders' catalogue.

When making a clock of this nature it is necessary to choose the movement first and adjust the dimensions of the case to fit the pendulum length and swing, front to back clearances of the movement and any chime assembly, and the drop required for the weights. All this information was given in the catalogue, or is available from Yorkshire Clock Builders who are very helpful, *see Suppliers*.

RIGHT: Clean Shaker-inspired lines and ripple sycamore give a light modern look to a traditional piece

Modifications

Because of the ceiling height of my cottage, the maximum height for my clock had to be 1980mm (78in) which was somewhat shorter than Mosers'. I also cut the front to back and side to side measurements pretty fine to give the slim, elegant look that I wanted – which resulted in a small footprint, which could give some instability in a piece of this height. Gripper rods at the edges of fitted carpets can also accentuate the problem by tending to tilt the clock forward.

"When making a clock of this nature it is necessary to choose the movement first and adjust the dimensions of the case to fit"

A clock maker I spoke to said that he always chocked the front of tall clocks to give a slight backwards lean for added safety, and Yorkshire Clock Builders confirmed that this would have no effect on the working of the movement. This 'lean back' feature was often built into Victorian tall book cases, the plinths being cut lower at the back so that the weight of the full book case was against the wall behind it.

I decided not to build the lean into the clock case but to chock the front with thin pieces of ply, which would have the advantage of being adjustable. The floors and walls in our cottage are not necessarily true!

Materials

I went to Duffield of Ripon, a timber merchant with whom I have dealt, almost exclusively, for many years, and chose some nice clean sycamore with a subtle figuring as the main timber for the case and bonnet, and some well figured ripple sycamore for the bonnet door frame and the edge of the lower case.

th the times

"A clock maker I spoke to said that he chocked the front of tall clocks to give a slight backwards lean for added safety"

All the sycamore and ripple sycamore, with the exception of the mouldings, is from boards finished to 19mm (¾in) thickness. The face board, to take the dial, is sycamore faced MDF, glued in all round for stability, as the spindle from the clock movement runs through it.

The backs of the lower case and bonnet are also sycamore faced MDF. The source of all my veneer faced MDF board is Spa Laminates of Leeds – they seem to have everything.

Construction
The front is made up from 50mm (2in) strips of ripple sycamore for the edges, and the centre from three pieces of sycamore, to make the top, door, and bottom pieces. All three pieces for the centre are cut from the same board so that the figure runs through.

The edges, and top and bottom centre pieces, are cut to size, edge planed, glued, and clamped-up leaving the door opening. Rebates are then cut in the edges to take the sides.

Sides
The sides are cut to size with the tops stepped back above the line of the top moulding, to run between the bottom braces of the bonnet. The sides protrude into the bonnet to finish just under the seat board rails.

Two housings are cut in the front and sides to take the base and the false base. The false base is necessary for bracing and strengthening, as the top is open. Its height above the base is dependent on the drop required for the weights.

The bases are both cut to size in solid timber with the grain running in the same direction as the sides. I use PVA glue when fitting them, and leave 3mm (⅛in) clearance in the depth of the housing in the sides, relying on the 'stretch' in PVA glue to provide sufficient give for movement across the grain on such a relatively short span.

The sides are morticed to take the top brace which is cut to size and tenoned to fit. The top brace, sides, as far as the false base, and the top of the false base, are slotted to take the sycamore faced MDF back, which is glued in all around.

The sides below the false base, the base, and underside of the false base are rebated to take the lower part of the back. This lower back is screwed into place so that it can be removed. A heavy weight could then be put inside the bottom of the clock to improve stability if needed. It turned out to be unnecessary in this case, but it might be a useful option.

All the pieces of the lower case are finished, dry fitted, then glued, clamped, checked for square, and left to dry.

Mouldings
The top and bottom mouldings are made and fitted with mitred corners using two different sizes of a simple cove profile. The actual profiles used are a matter of personal taste and the cutters you have for your router, spindle moulder, or moulding plane!

The mouldings are screwed from the inside using double counter sunk holes to allow for movement.

"The actual profiles used are a matter of personal taste and the cutters you have for your router, spindle moulder, or moulding plane!"

ABOVE: Simple clock face and mouldings continue the clean lines

BELOW: Double countersunk screws allow for movement as in the door braces

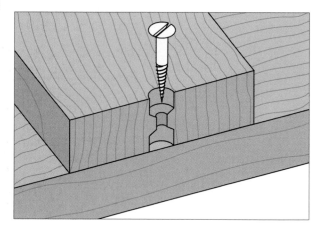

"All three pieces for the centre are cut from the same board so that the figure runs through"

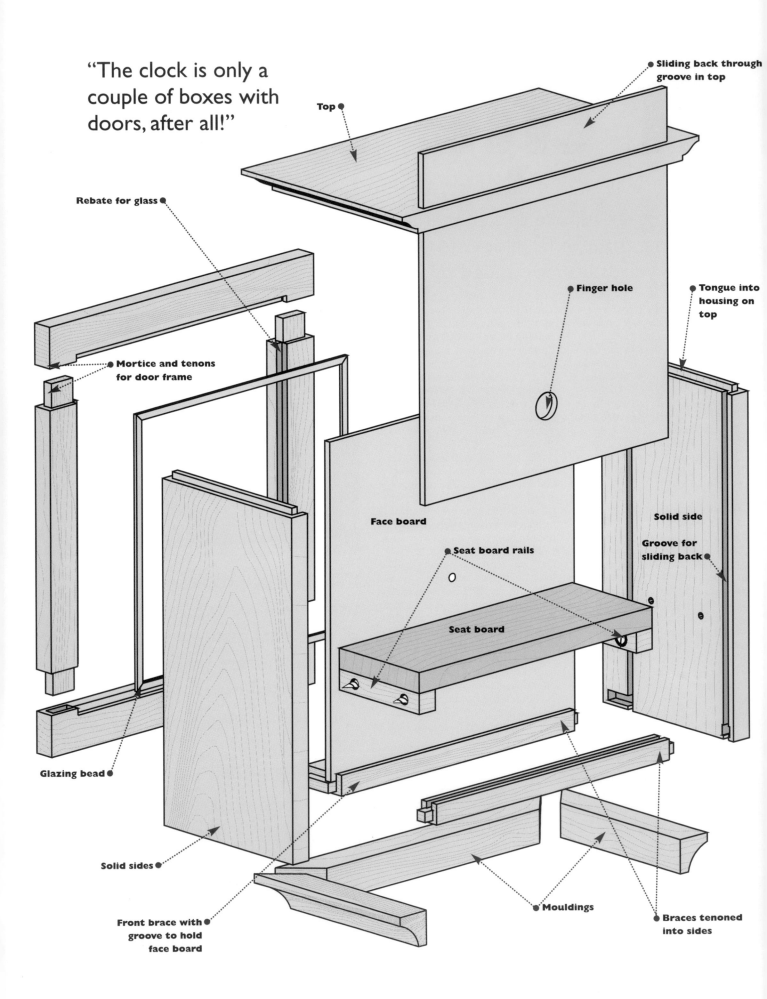

"The clock is only a couple of boxes with doors, after all!"

Sliding back through groove in top

Top

Rebate for glass

Finger hole

Tongue into housing on top

Mortice and tenons for door frame

Face board

Solid side

Seat board rails

Groove for sliding back

Seat board

Glazing bead

Solid sides

Mouldings

Front brace with groove to hold face board

Braces tenoned into sides

Door

The door is a simple construction of a single board with an internal brace top and bottom. The edges of the braces are rounded over to a 6mm (¼in) radius, and are screwed to the door, again in double counter sunk holes – but this time the holes are plugged.

The turn catch is also a Shaker design which I made in fumed oak to give a little contrast to the front. The door stops are fitted inside the case at the top and bottom of the opening. It is worth noting that everyone who gets close enough to this clock will want to open it to see the 'works'. Make sure the turn catch is strong enough to take the initial pull before they realise that a turn is required!

> "It is worth noting that everyone who gets close enough to this clock will want to open it to see the 'works'!"

Bonnet

The bonnet top is cut to size, housings cut for the sides, and an ogee moulding formed on the front and side edges. A stopped slot is cut for the sliding back and a stopped housing for the face board.

The sides are cut to size and housings cut for the back and face board. The bottoms are morticed for the braces, and the tops shouldered back 6mm (¼in) to fit the stopped housings in the top. The seat board

rails are screwed on, in double countersunk holes.

The braces are cut to size and tenoned to fit the pre-cut mortices. Housings are cut for the face board and back.

All the parts are finished and dry fitted, then glued and clamped, checked for square, and left to dry. A piece of sycamore faced MDF is cut to size and fitted as the sliding back, in which I drilled a 25mm (1in) finger hole to assist opening.

Bonnet door

The door frame is made from ripple sycamore to frame the face. I did not want anything to break the line, so I used a magnetic button catch behind the frame, and recessed 38mm (1½in) brass butt hinges as far in as possible.

The frame pieces are cut to size, the top and bottom rails morticed, and the side rails tenoned to fit. Rebates are cut on the inside of the frame for the glass and glazing bead. The glass is fitted into the frame on a thin bed of clear silicone mastic, the glazing bead pinned into position, and the pins counter sunk and filled.

The door is then fitted to the bonnet, the bonnet to the lower case, and any necessary adjustments are made.

Finish

I decided to finish the clock before finally fitting the movement – but I did do a dry run first to check that everything fitted! To keep the whiteness of the sycamore I chose a satin finish, water based, acrylic varnish with a UV filter. I applied three coats with a sponge, rubbing down between coats to denib, and finished with two coats of clear wax.

ABOVE: Simplicity is the key to this door and latch
BELOW: Sliding back for time adjustments, note carcass sides locking into bonnet, and side board rails

MOVEMENT

The bonnet is removed from the lower case and the door and back from the bonnet. The movement seat board is cut from 13mm (1/2in) ply to the detailed dimensions provided with the movement, and screwed to the rails inside the bonnet.

The movement is offered to the back of the face board, and the position for the hand's spindle is marked. A hole is drilled for the spindle and, using this to locate the face, it is glued to the face board with one of the 'I can't believe it's not nails' glues.

The detailed fitting and adjustment of the movement is not complicated or difficult and full instructions are provided with the movement from the Yorkshire Clock Builders. It would be worth checking that the supplier you use does provide the instructions for fitting, and is willing to give advice if required.

I found it relatively easy to adjust the clock to an accuracy of +/- 10 seconds a week. There are several choices of movement for this type of clock. A battery driven quartz movement with false weights and a moving pendulum is available.

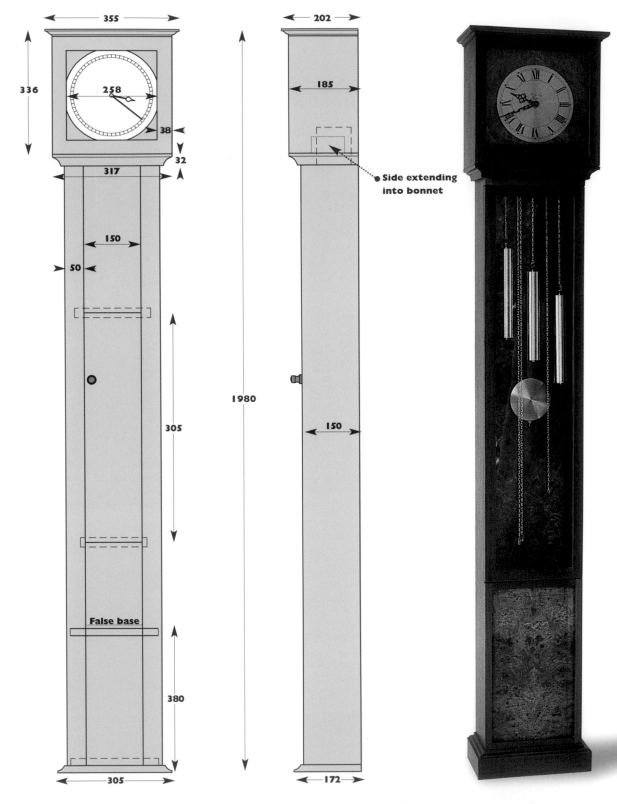

Side extending
into bonnet

Conclusion

I enjoyed making this clock – and it has attracted much
favourable comment, and sales. I used the basic design for a
more ornamental version in oiled mahogany (*Swietenia spp*) and
burr elm (*Ulmus spp*) with a glazed lower door and a full
Westminster chime.

There seems to be some mystique about these long case
clocks – people viewing my work, in the full knowledge of
what I do for a living, are surprised that I made the clock, but
not surprised that I made a chair with compound joints,
contrasting inlays, and steam bent arms. The clock is only a
couple of boxes with doors, after all!

Enjoy the project and its disproportionate effort and praise ratio! ■

ABOVE RIGHT:
More ornamental
version in oiled
mahogany and
burr elm

"There seems to be some
mystique about these long
case clocks – people are
surprised that I made it, but
not surprised that I made a
chair with compound joints,
contrasting inlays, and
steam bent arms!"

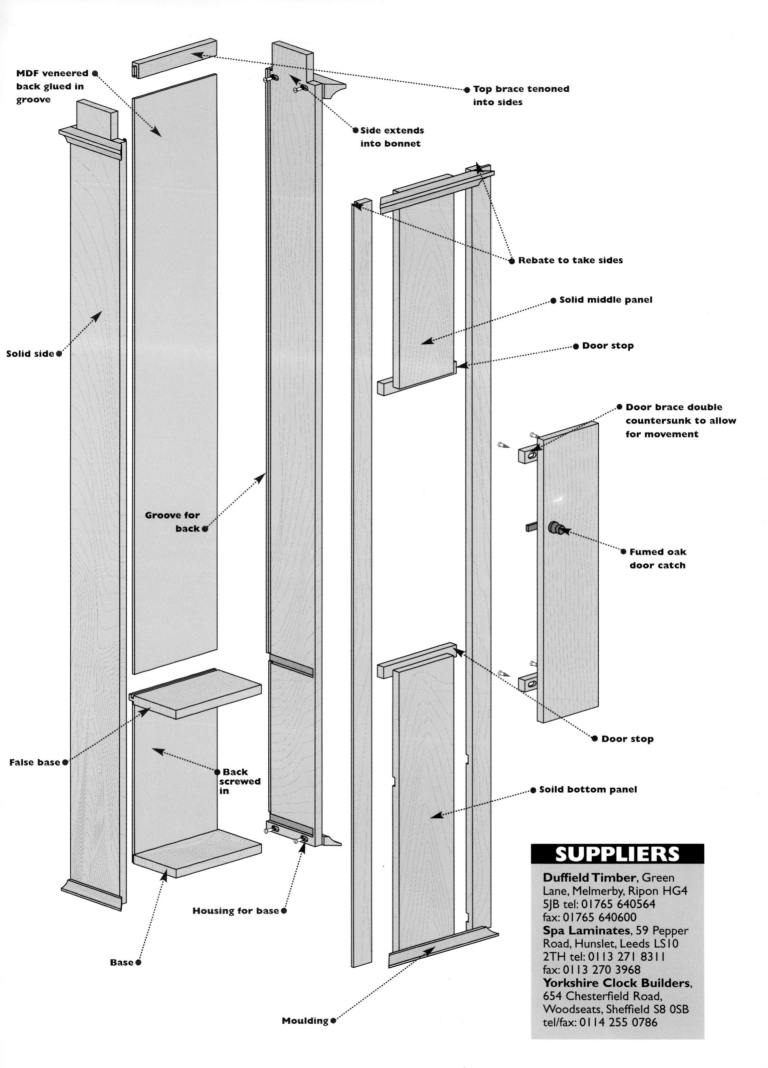

MDF veneered● back glued in groove

● Top brace tenoned into sides

● Side extends into bonnet

● Rebate to take sides

● Solid middle panel

● Door stop

Solid side●

Groove for back●

● Door brace double countersunk to allow for movement

● Fumed oak door catch

False base●

● Back screwed in

● Door stop

● Soild bottom panel

Housing for base●

Base●

Moulding●

SUPPLIERS

Duffield Timber, Green Lane, Melmerby, Ripon HG4 5JB tel: 01765 640564 fax: 01765 640600
Spa Laminates, 59 Pepper Road, Hunslet, Leeds LS10 2TH tel: 0113 271 8311 fax: 0113 270 3968
Yorkshire Clock Builders, 654 Chesterfield Road, Woodseats, Sheffield S8 0SB tel/fax: 0114 255 0786

Vision On!

How to make a TV cabinet in elm and burr elm

MANY PEOPLE enjoy watching television while it is on, but when it's turned off, they find that it becomes an unsightly piece of equipment that dominates the room. A purpose-built cabinet is one way to disguise the television, video and hi-fi, and it can be designed to fit in with the decor.

Obviously each cabinet needs to be tailored to fit the individual pieces of equipment. With the choice of such hardware being so large, it is difficult for a furniture manufacturer to provide a broad enough range of cabinets to house them – what they do produce tends to be on the large side, on the grounds that you can put a small television in a big cabinet! Luckily for bespoke makers, many people find this an unsatisfactory solution!

"One important thing to remember when designing the cabinet is the heat generated by these appliances"

Design

I made this cabinet some years ago to house our TV and video. The requirements were simple – a cupboard to hold the equipment, and a drawer underneath for cassettes and programmes, and it was to have a Georgian feel so that it would blend in with the style of our cottage.

One important thing to remember when designing the cabinet is the heat generated by these appliances – a good circulation of air is essential. The tube of a television overhangs at the back, making the depth much more than you would think. In this case the cabinet was to stand in a corner so I decided to have no back at all in it. The back of the tube projects into the dead space behind the cabinet, thus reducing the cabinet depth and allowing for a good circulation of air.

Construction

The top is made up from two pieces of elm (*Ulmus spp*) that had some nice 'cat's paw' markings. The boards are selected and positioned so that the figure runs through the join. When jointing up important pieces to increase the width I carefully match

"The cabinet was to stand in a corner so I decided to have no back at all in it"

LEFT: Cabinet in
elm and burr elm
– and the TV
discreetly
disappears

"It was marked out well oversize and the whole lot went into the kiln for a month"

the grain direction and colour, and ensure that the figure runs through to disguise the join.

The edges are planed straight and flat on the surface planer, then finished with a jointing plane to take out the ripples, and the centre of the join is planed slightly hollow.

When the pieces are clamped-up, the ends are under slight pressure, which compensates for the extra shrinkage caused by faster drying at the ends through the end-grain. I reinforce the join with a loose tongue, *see fig 1*, or nowadays, a number of biscuits.

BELOW: Fig 1 Traditional sprung joint

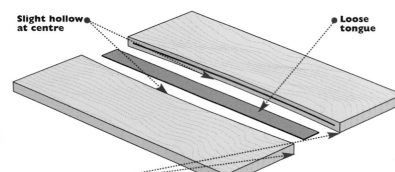

Slight hollow
at centre

Loose
tongue

Tight fit at ends

TIMBER SELECTION

I had some nice elm from a tree which had come down in our field, and some burr which I had scavenged from the local hedgerows. Both had been boarded to a generous 25mm (1in) thickness, sticked and air-dried for a couple of years inside my wood store.

As is often the case with elm left standing after the ravages of Dutch elm disease, there was some insect damage. This I had treated with a Cuprinol insecticide which comes in a pressurised can and can be squirted into the holes. I always have a long-term insect-killer in the wood-store and workshop as a general precaution. For safety's sake I repeated the insecticide treatment before the wood went into my kiln, see *Coping with stress*, page 7, and *Turning up the heat*, page 11.

Selecting the elm was reasonably straightforward. I inspected it carefully, cutting out all areas with insect damage, and marking it out well oversize, allowing for unseen defects. The nicest piece was earmarked for the top as it would be seen the most.

The burr was more difficult as I didn't have much to choose from in the sizes I needed. To check the likely final colour I gave it a coat of white spirit to approximate a varnish finish. Again, it was marked out well oversize and the whole lot went into the kiln for a month.

Sides, base and shelf

The sides, base and shelf are similarly made up, clamped, left to dry and then cut to size.

A slot is cut in the shelf, base and bottom of the sides to take a 5mm (3/16in) ply back to the bottom part of the cabinet behind the drawer. Leaving the back out of the top of the cabinet significantly weakens it, especially when one considers the likely weight of the contents. I was anxious to gain all the strength I could by gluing this back in all around.

Next the housings are cut in the sides to take the shelf and base. All these pieces are finished down to 240 grit and dry-fitted, then glue is applied to all the housings, and clamped, checked for square, and left to set.

The edges of the top are rounded-over to 6mm (1/4in) radius and the

"It worked quite well – there was little movement and the width of the shadow-line did not change – but I was lucky"

housings cut to take the sides. The top is then finished, fitted and clamped. The whole piece is finally checked for square and left to set.

Plinth

The top edge of the plinth is shaped on the router using an ovolo cutter. The front and sides are cut to size and the front corners mitred. The bottom edge is shaped by drilling interlocking 25mm (1in) holes and joining them up with a jigsaw.

The edge is finished with a plane and scraper, and then sanded. The front of the plinth is glued and screwed from the back onto the supporting strip. Glue is applied to the mitre join and the first 75mm (3in) of the plinth sides, which are clamped into position. The remainder of the plinth sides are left dry and fixed at the back to the side of the cabinet, through an oversize hole with a screw and washer. This is to allow for any movement across the grain in the sides.

Doors

The door frames of the cabinet are made from 50mm by 22mm (2in by 7/8in) elm, morticed and tenoned in the usual way. I cut the tenons exactly off the saw, as any adjustment with a plane tends to make them very vulnerable to introducing wind.

The burr panels are made from boards split down the middle and joined up, as in a book matched veneer. Unfortunately the boards I had were not sequential, and the panels did not quite match. I decided, after much deliberation, that they looked better un-matched with

one upside down, rather than matched-but-not-quite!

The panels are rebated into slots in the door frame with 3mm (1/8in) clearance around the edge to allow for movement and provide a shadow-line around the edge of the burr. It worked quite well – there was little movement and the width of the shadow-line did not change – but I was lucky – I wouldn't use this method again, traditional fielded panels are safer.

The doors are fitted with brass butt hinges, brassed magnetic catches under the top, and antiqued drop brass pulls from Savill's.

Drawer

The drawer casings are made from sweet chestnut (*Castanea sativa*) and the front from solid burr, which are dovetailed back and front.

The base is from oak-faced MDF let into the sides and front, screwed

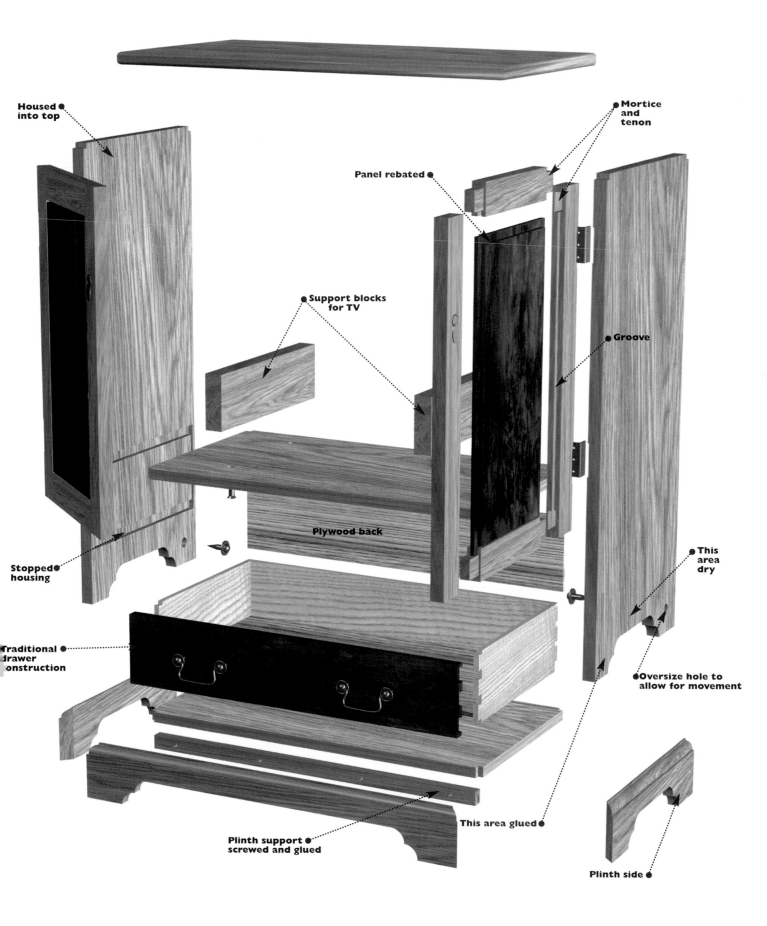

Housed into top

Mortice and tenon

Panel rebated

Support blocks for TV

Groove

Stopped housing

This area dry

Traditional drawer construction

Plywood back

Oversize hole to allow for movement

This area glued

Plinth support screwed and glued

Plinth side

to the back, and glued all around for strength. I kept the tools extra-sharp when dovetailing the burr – and the Superglue was handy, just in case.

The drawer front is given a little more clearance to allow for the extra movement which can be expected from burr. Antiqued brass handles are fitted to match the drop handles on the doors.

"I kept the tools extra-sharp when dovetailing the burr – and the Superglue was handy, just in case"

Conclusion

I decided not to have a shelf over the video recorder to stand the television on so as to give as much flexibility as possible in the event of a change of equipment. However, I decided to add support blocks to take the weight. These were screwed through from inside the drawer compartment and are not obtrusive.

About 30 minutes after the television is switched on there is a distinct creak as something in the construction reacts to the change of temperature! I have been unable to find what or where, but the cabinet is still standing and functioning well.

Obviously the measurements given are specific to our TV and video and adjustments would need to be made for individual equipment. I would suggest 25mm (1in) clearance all around for airflow and ease of fitting. Beware wide screen and digital TV ! ∎

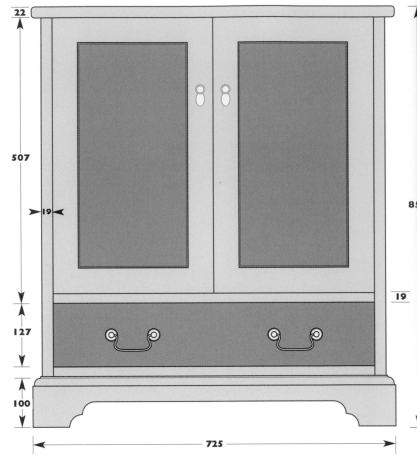

RIGHT: Interior detail showing TV support blocks

FINISH

Everything is checked carefully for clamping marks, glue-ooze, and minor defects and then hand-sanded with 240 and 320 grit. Two coats of sanding sealer are applied and each rubbed down with 320 grit. Then, three coats of satin polyurethane varnish, diluted with ⅓ white spirit, are applied with a pad. Each coat is given 24 hours drying time in a warm, dry, workshop, and then de-nibbed before application of the next coat. The last coat is buffed with a Scotchbrite grey pad and given two coats of wax.

SUPPLIERS

H.E. Savill, Period Cabinet Fittings, 9 St. Martin's Place, Scarborough, North Yorkshire, WO11 2QH. Tel: 01723 373032

On the case

How to make bookcases in brown oak and sycamore

ILLUSTRATIONS BY SIMON RODWAY

These bookcases were made for a regular client who also commissioned four partners' desks (see pages 50 and 56). They were ordered at the same time as the desks so the planning and design was done before my move from Yorkshire to Shropshire. The actual making was done some time later so the time lapse and the distance from the client made careful notes and measurements essential!

Design

The client lives in a beautiful market town in the upper reaches of Teesdale in North Yorkshire. His substantial 18th century house is of traditional, solid stone construction with good-sized rooms. The bookcases were to go one each side of the chimney breast in the sitting room, which is well-proportioned with a bay window and high ceiling.

A simple honest design in solid wood seemed to be most sympathetic to the surroundings. For flexibility of use, movement, and construction, we

The ripple
sycamore doors give
these traditional bookcases
a more contemporary feel

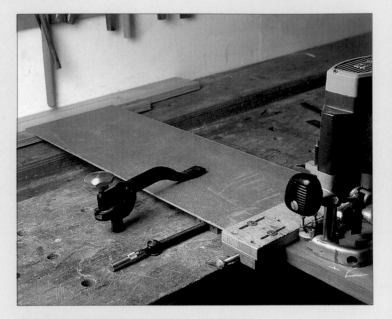

Simple jig for routing the housings for the shelves

"The bookcases were to go one each side of the chimney breast in the sitting room, which is well-proportioned with a bay window and high ceiling"

Top components masked up, ready for finishing

decided to make each bookcase in two pieces, with a shallower top cupboard sitting on a deeper base.

During our discussions about the desks, my client had been taken with some brown oak samples I had shown him, and decided he would like the bookcases made in that. I thought that they might look a bit heavy and dull and so I suggested sycamore shelves and back to lighten things up. Having decided on glazed doors to reduce dusting, we carried this theme a bit further and went for ripple sycamore door frames.

Weight of books

I hate making bookcases with adjustable shelves – the structure is weakened and the shelves are rarely moved after the initial loading. Far better to line up all the books which are to go in it and work out the shelf spacings required beforehand, allowing much stronger, permanent shelf fixing. The client agreed and did just that.

A full bookcase, particularly of this size, holds a considerable weight of books. I always impress on clients that bookcases should only be moved when empty!

Bearing in mind the weight of the books and the height of the pieces, I wanted to use the 'lean back' feature often built into Victorian tall bookcases. Then the plinths were cut lower at the back so that the weight of the full bookcase was against the wall behind it.

I decided not to build the lean into the cabinet but to chock it as required – this would have the advantage of being adjustable to the floor and walls in the house which were unlikely to be exactly true and level, having regard to its age.

Environment

The floor was carpeted and had 'gripper' edging strip under the carpet, against the skirting, which would tend to lift the back the wrong way, so this would also have to be allowed for.

The skirting boards were original –

10in high and 1½in thick. An overhang was built into the back of the top of the base units so that the top unit would still be against the wall.

To prevent the top unit being pulled forward in use, a metal bracket was screwed to the back of the top unit and the underside of the base unit top.

I retired to the computer to produce the drawing, check availability of materials, and cost up the job. Once all was approved, I set off to secure my supplies.

Timber selection

I had checked with my usual timber merchant that brown oak and ripple sycamore were available, but I wanted to select the boards and arrange to have it delivered to my timber store in Shropshire in due course. I selected some nice quarter-sawn brown oak of even colour with few faults, and some clean sycamore and ripple sycamore.

Even though I know my timber merchant is very careful about their

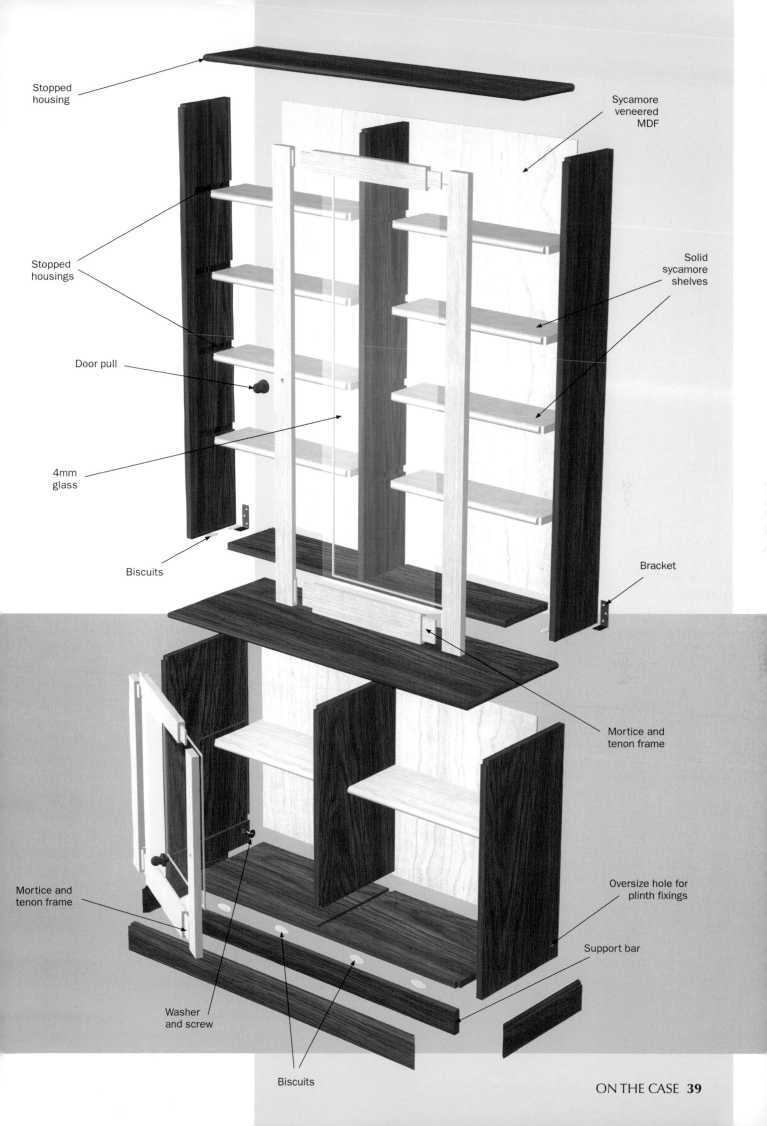

Stopped housing

Stopped housings

Door pull

4mm glass

Biscuits

Sycamore veneered MDF

Solid sycamore shelves

Bracket

Mortice and tenon frame

Mortice and tenon frame

Washer and screw

Biscuits

Oversize hole for plinth fixings

Support bar

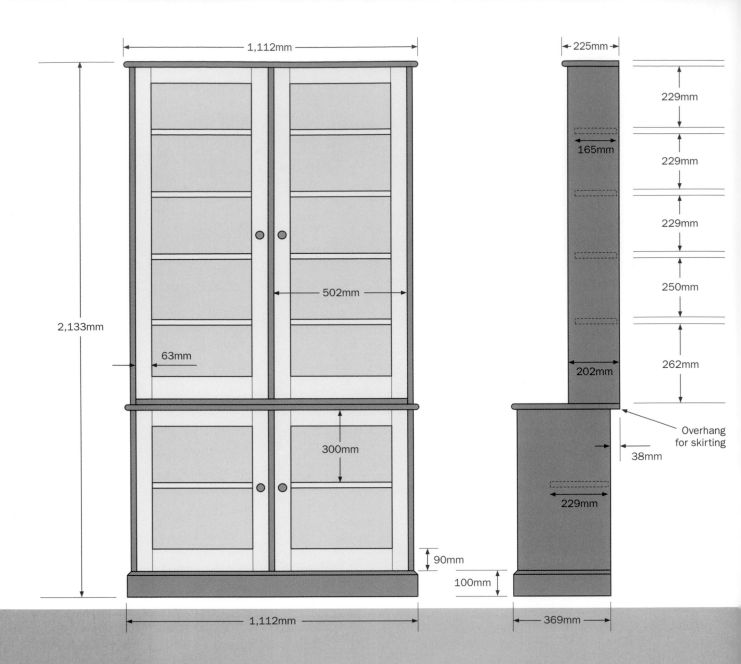

sycamore, I checked that it had been end-reared and used a plane to see that the stick marks did not penetrate too far. The sycamore-faced MDF for the backs was ordered later through a local Shropshire timber merchant.

Once I had moved to Shropshire and built my new timber store with its de-humidifier, I arranged delivery of the timber in plenty of time to condition it properly before use.

Timber preparation

The boards I had selected were of suitable dimensions and such quality that there was little wastage – this timber was not cheap! The components were marked out and cut over-size, sticked and left for some weeks to settle in the timber store.

Conditions in the new timber store are excellent and any final conditioning takes place during making in the workshop. The importance of correct

conditions for timber storage and furniture-making cannot be over-emphasised. The closer the temperature and humidity in the workshop are to the end-use destination, the better.

Carcass construction

All the components are thicknessed to 22mm (⅞in), then the plinth pieces reduced to 16mm (⅝in). All are cut to width and length, carefully checking accuracy before making so many repeat cuts! My work-space was organised so that the components could be sticked and stacked flat during making, with free air-flow to all faces for even drying.

The 5mm (¼in), sycamore-faced, MDF backs were also cut to size.

Housings

Stopped housings for the shelves, 22mm (⅞in) wide by 10mm (⅜in) deep, are cut with a router in the sides and partitions.

Similar stopped housings are cut in the tops to take the sides and the partitions, and in the bases of the top and bottom units to take the partitions. Housings are also cut in the sides of the bottom units to take the bases. The bases of the top units are fitted with biscuits.

As there are so many repeat cuts to the same spacing, I made a measuring jig out of hardboard and a batten to position my home-made router guide.

A slot is cut in the sides and tops, 5mm (¼in) wide by 5mm (¼in) deep, to take the backs – the front face of the backs being 10mm (⅜in) in from the back edge of the sides.

The sides, partitions, shelves, and bases of the bottom units are all shouldered and dry-fitted into their respective housings. Then the front edges of the shelves, and the front and side edges of the tops, are rounded over to 10mm (⅜in) radius.

Top cramped up

The plinth is biscuit jointed

Base with doors open

Internal finish

The sycamore shelves and backs are finished with an acrylic varnish containing a UV filter to preserve the pale colour and give a silky smooth feel. The oak, on the other hand, is oiled to enhance its deep brown colour, and the contrast of the coarser, open-grained surface.

In order not to contaminate the glue joint, the housings and the ends of the shelves, partitions, and sides are masked off and the internal surfaces finished. The oak is given three coats of Danish oil, each left 24 hours, and rubbed down between coats to de-nib – the sycamore is given three coats of acrylic, water-based, satin-finish varnish, also rubbed down between coats.

Assembly

Once the finishes have cured, each carcass is trial assembled dry. There was a problem with clamping where the partition fitted to the base, so as that face would not be visible in use, so I

decided to glue and screw that joint. The screws would be counter-sunk through the base and the holes plugged later.

The only difference in the assembly of the top and bottom units is that the base of the top unit is biscuited into position, and the base of the bottom unit housed like the shelves.

In all cases, glue is brushed into the housings, the partition fitted to the base, and screwed into position. Then the base is fitted to the sides, and the shelves fitted into the housings in the sides and partitions. Clamps are applied, diagonals measured to check that all is square, and the unit left to set.

The housings in the relevant top are glued and the top clamped into position on the sides, the carcass unit again checked for square, and left to set.

Backs

Glue is applied to the back edges of the shelves, partition, and base, and the

slots in the sides and tops, then the pre-finished back is placed carefully in position and screwed through to the shelves, partition and base. It is a fiddly job to glue and screw the backs in this way but is worth it for the extra strength. The processes are repeated until both top and both base-units are assembled.

Plinths

A support bar for the plinth front is fitted between the sides of each base unit, screwed through the sides and biscuited to the base above it.

The plinth pieces are given an ogee moulding on the top edge with a router, cut to length, and mitred on the radial arm saw. I used a negative rake, cross-cut blade for finish and prevention of 'climbing' over the work – adjustments were made by hand, on the shooting board.

Biscuits are used in the mitres – very useful in preventing them slipping when they are clamped up, apart

Top with doors open

The completed pair of bookcases

> *"The importance of correct conditions for timber storage and furniture-making cannot be over-emphasised"*

from the obvious benefit of the extra strength.

The plinth front is fitted by screwing and gluing, from the back, on to the support bar. Aliphatic resin glue is applied to the mitres for a really strong joint with no 'creep'. The first 75mm (3in) of the plinth sides are also glued to the sides, this time with PVA, which allows a little movement, and clamped into position. The remainder of the plinth sides are left dry. They are fixed at the back, from the inside, through an oversize hole, with a screw and washer. This allows for any movement in the sides, across the grain.

The mitres are tapped over where necessary and sanded finished when dry.

Doors

The ripple sycamore door frame pieces are cut to size, the top and bottom rails tenoned, and the stiles morticed to fit. Rebates are cut, with a router, on the inside of the frame for the glass and glazing bead. The glazing bead

is cut to size and fitted. The unglazed door frames are carefully fitted in the usual way with brass butt hinges and ball catches, then removed and finished with 3 coats of acrylic varnish before glazing.

The 4mm (⅛in) glass is fitted into the frame on a very thin bed of clear silicone mastic, the glazing bead is pre-drilled and pinned into position, the pins counter-sunk and filled. Door pulls are turned from brown oak, and fitted with screwed dowels.

Finish

Most of the finishing has been completed during construction, so all that remains is to sand the outside of the carcasses, remove any clamping or other marks, and apply several coats of Danish oil. All the other finished surfaces are checked and any marks removed. There is always a danger of marking the surface if the finishing has to take place before the end, so to speak. Once all is clean and cured, the doors

are fitted and any minor adjustments made. Then two coats of wax are applied to all surfaces and buffed up to a nice sheen.

Delivery

The finished items were delivered to Teesdale as a part-load on a furniture wagon and I went up to assemble them. The floor wasn't quite level and the walls weren't quite true, but some judicious hidden chocks took care of it! I did manage to get them to lean back slightly against the wall behind.

Conclusion

Though large, the bookcases are of relatively simple construction with a lot of repetitive work, to which I applied the lessons learned when making the four partners' desks. I liked the blend of brown oak with the sycamores and felt the different finishes worked particularly well. My client was pleased, and that is the name of the game! ■

Seven

How to make an Arts and Crafts-style seven-drawer chest

WHEN WE MOVED from Yorkshire to Shropshire, the study in our new cottage had a limited floor area compared to what we were used to. There were several ways I devised to utilise the space well – one way was to make the hanging corner cupboard on page 105, and another answer was this seven-drawer chest – its main function being to store display and exhibition paraphernalia and office supplies.

Design

When making furniture for myself, I feel it should also be used for display and, of course, it gives me the opportunity for a little experimentation!

I decided to go for an Arts and Crafts look to this piece. As the main item in the study is a partner's desk in fumed oak and sycamore, I kept to the theme but reversed the accent by having the fumed oak framed by the sycamore, instead of vice versa. The drawer arrangement was based on a chest I had made for a previous client but with the draw depth and width increased to take A3 paper.

The visible through-dovetails in the top and sides are typical of the genre and were accentuated by the contrasting woods, as were the drawer dovetails. I came up with the shaped rather than turned drawer pulls, again in contrasting woods, to provide just the sort of detail to complete the look I wanted.

The plinth shape was developed from a Gordon Russell design shown in Alan Peters' excellent book *Cabinetmaking – the Professional Approach*, which contains much useful information about the craft movement in English furniture.

Carcass construction

The sides are made up first, each from two widths of sycamore. The figure is matched carefully and the joint strengthened with a ply loose tongue. The edges are planed on the surfacer and finished by hand to remove the ripples – made slightly

RIGHT: Arts and Crafts-inspired chest developed from earlier pieces

INSPIRATION

One winter's day, some time ago when I first started my workshop, a formidable lady and her husband visited me unannounced, having read an article about me published in a woodworking magazine.

After a full inspection of my work and premises, and addressing me as 'young man', she invited me to her house some distance away to see her collection of Arts and Crafts furniture.

A week or so later I went – and was treated to a splendid display of museum-quality English oak and walnut Arts and Crafts furniture, in a house built by her architect son, with the furniture in mind. Tea and cakes were served at a fine Arts and Crafts table with matching chairs – a feast for the body and the soul.

I fell in love with the quality and honesty of the construction, the simplicity of line, and the careful selection and use of timber. My generous host gave me a book on Charles Rennie Macintosh as a parting gift. Sadly, I lost her address and have never see her again, but she had quite an influence on my subsequent career.

hollow in the middle, so that the ends are under pressure, which allows for the extra shrinkage as the end-grain loses water more quickly.

A 10mm deep by 5mm wide (⅜ by ³⁄₁₆in) slot is cut in the sides for the MDF back. The end of this slot will be covered by the top dovetail. The top frame stopped housing, 10mm by 10mm (⅜in by ⅜in), is offset down to leave room for the top dovetails – then the 19mm wide by 10mm deep (¾in by ⅜in) stopped housings for the remaining drawer frames are cut.

The drawer frames are made up from 50mm by 19mm (2in by ¾in) sycamore with mortice and tenon joints, and shouldered front and back to go into the stopped housings. The front mortice and tenons are glued but the back joints are left dry with an expansion gap to allow for movement in the sides.

The top frame sides are rebated to 10mm (⅜in) for the offset top housing. The carcass pieces are finished as far as possible, fitted and clamped-up dry.

Top

The top is also made up from two pieces, similar to the sides, but of oak. When dry, it is cut exactly to size.

An allowance is made in the dovetails so that the tails and pins are slightly proud when fully driven home. The dovetail pins are marked in the top, the majority of the waste is removed on the bandsaw – they are then chiselled to size, and finished by hand.

Next, the top is offered up to the dry-clamped carcass and the tails marked. The carcass is dismantled and the tails on the top of the sides cut by hand with a dovetail saw and chiselled out on the bench. With the carcass re-assembled dry and clamped, the top is tapped home about 3mm (⅛in) to check the fit (dovetails only go together once!) and then carefully removed.

A stopped slot 10mm by 5mm (⅜in by ³⁄₁₆in) is cut in the top to take the back. The carcass is assembled with the drawer frames glued into the housings in the front and back of the carcass sides, leaving the sides of the frames a dry running fit in the sides of the carcass to allow for future movement.

The back is dryfitted to help keep it square. Clamps are applied, the diagonals measured front and back to check it is square, adjustments are

made, and it is left to set.

Plinth

The plinth pieces are dressed to 16mm (⅝in) thickness from the oak and cut to size. The top edge is shaped with an ogee cutter on the router, and the mitre cut on the front edges. The plinth is then dryfitted with clamps to check the fit.

Drawers

The drawer fronts and casings are cut to size. The fronts are made from 22mm (⅞in) oak, and the remainder of the casings from 10mm (⅜in) sycamore to give a strong contrast to the dovetails. The bases are from sycamore-faced MDF glued in all round to add strength. The tails are cut out undersize on the bandsaw and finished to size with a paring chisel. The majority of the waste for the pins are removed with a router and, again, they are finished with a sharp paring chisel.

ABOVE: Partner's desk in fumed oak and sycamore provided the theme

FAR LEFT: An earlier chest of drawers suggested the drawer arrangement

BELOW LEFT: Exposed joints are accentuated by the contrasting woods

BELOW: Fine tail detail

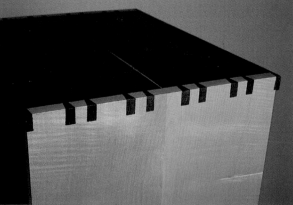

TIMBER CHOICE

The top and drawer fronts were to be finished to 22mm (⅞in) so I chose some 28mm (1³⁄₃₂in) quarter sawn French oak with straight grain and good figure. I also found some nice clean English sycamore for the sides, drawer rails, and casings.

All the timber was bought as kiln dried but, as usual, it was initially cut over-size, sticked, and conditioned in my home-made kiln. After a couple of weeks it was machined to final size and kept in my warm workshop, still in stick, throughout the making process.

ABOVE RIGHT: Plinth design was developed from a Gordon Russell design

Fuming

Sycamore reacts to the fuming process by going a greyish colour so it is necessary to fume all the oak pieces separately, prior to construction.

Now that the top plinth pieces and drawer fronts are finished to exact sizes with the joints cut, they are all fumed. The pieces are wiped over with white spirit to show any marks – which are then removed – they are then left to dry, and hand-sanded to 320 grit.

I use a temporary polythene tent and some saucers of 880 ammonia for the fuming and leave the pieces – all standing on an edge which will not be seen – for 24 hours. This process must be undertaken with

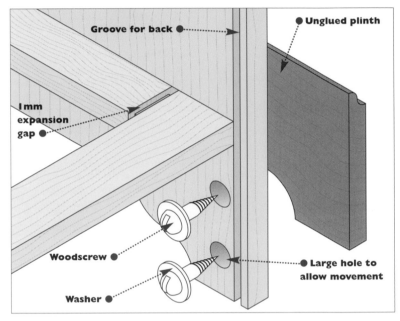

Labels: Groove for back • ; • Unglued plint; 1mm expansion gap •; Woodscrew •; Washer •; • Large hole to allow movement

DRAWER PULLS

The drawer pulls are made up from strips of pre-fumed oak, and sycamore. The blanks are made long enough to make two pulls by cutting out the middle section on the bandsaw which makes them easier and safer to handle. Again, I used Aliphatic resin glue for a really strong joint.

After cutting out on the bandsaw, the pulls are finished with a small block plane. Any attempt to sand them results in the transfer of fumed oak dust to the sycamore, discolouring it.

The pulls are drilled and wood to wood, double-ended dowel screws inserted. Apply epoxy resin glue to the thread going into the pull so that it is fixed at the correct depth.

Construction of drawer pulls

Drawer pulls are fixed with double ended screws and Araldite

care and eye protection should be worn – ammonia has a particularly adverse effect on the eyes and contact causes permanent damage.

Assembly

With the fuming complete, glue is applied to the top dovetails and the top driven down with a hammer and wooden block. The block is offset slightly to allow the tails to protrude by the small amount allowed for.

After the top has set, the plinth is fitted by screwing and gluing the front, from the back, on to the supporting strip. Aliphatic resin glue is applied to the mitre joints for a really strong joint with no 'creep'. The first 75mm (3in) of the plinth sides are also glued, this time with PVA which allows a little movement, and clamped into position. The remainder of the plinth sides are left dry. They are fixed at the back to the side of the cabinet, from the inside, through an oversize hole, with a screw and washer. This allows for any movement in the sides, across the grain.

The drawers are assembled, checked for square and wind, and left to set. They are then fitted in the usual way, before gluing the back into place.

Finish

The top dovetails are sanded flush. Sanding the proud fumed oak pins makes no difference to the colour as the fuming penetrates deeply into the end grain. Care should be taken when sanding the tops of the tails so as not to sand into the fumed oak top.

The remainder of the cabinet is checked carefully for glue ooze, marks and blemishes, then hand-sanded with 320 grit.

I usually finish fumed oak with oil to deepen the colour, and sycamore with acrylic varnish to preserve its pale hue. However, as the final finishing of the top dovetails could not take place until after assembly, acrylic varnish is applied overall, then two coats of wax, buffed to a nice sheen. The result is pleasing, with a little lightening effect on the oak.

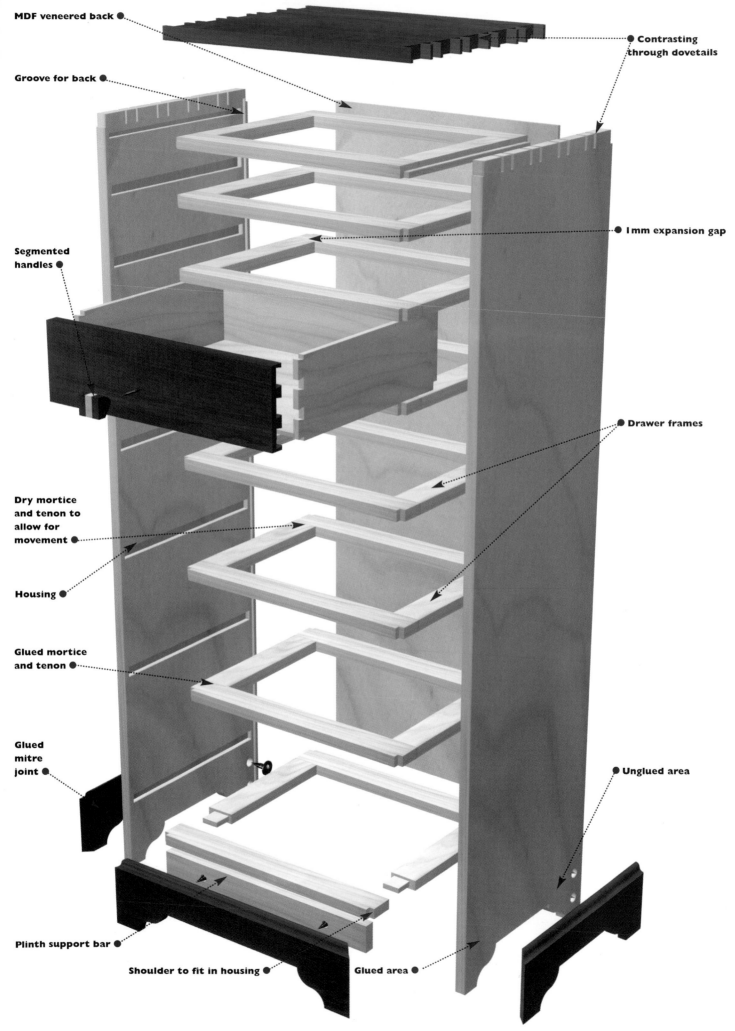

MDF veneered back ●

Contrasting through dovetails ●

Groove for back ●

1mm expansion gap ●

Segmented handles ●

Drawer frames ●

Dry mortice and tenon to allow for movement ●

Housing ●

Glued mortice and tenon ●

Glued mitre joint ●

Unglued area ●

Plinth support bar ●

Shoulder to fit in housing ●

Glued area ●

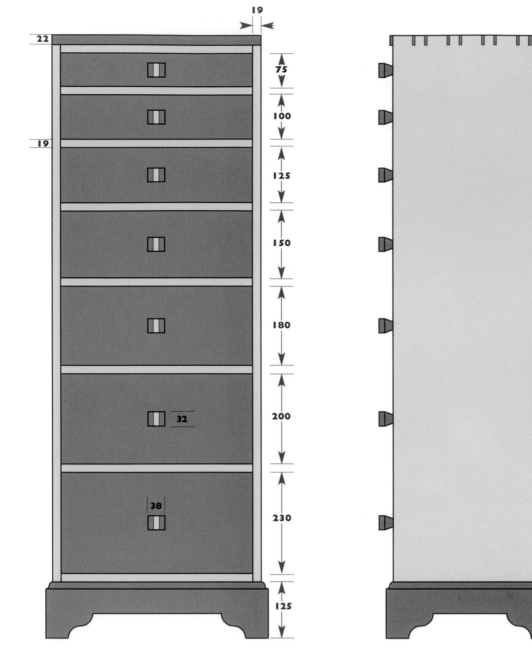

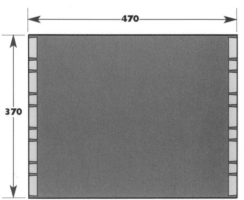

> "The visible through-dovetails in the top and sides are typical of the genre and were accentuated by the contrasting woods, as were the drawer dovetails"

Conclusion

I particularly enjoy making dovetails and this piece gave me the opportunity to show them off as a feature in contrasting woods! Overall I felt that it achieved its aim as a functional, unusual piece, with an Arts and Crafts influence. ■

SUPPLIERS

Craft Supplies Ltd, The Mill, Millers Dale, Nr Buxton, Derbyshire, SK17 8SN Tel: 01298 871636

Screwfix Direct, Freepost, Yeovil, BA22 8BF Tel: 0500 414141

REFERENCES

Cabinetmaking – the Professional Approach by Alan Peters, published by Stobart & Son Ltd.

ISBN 0 85442 024X

Two of a kind

MAIN ILLUSTRATION BY IAN HALL

In a two-part project you can make four partners' desks

ABOVE RIGHT:
First variation, with cupboards in the centre

BELOW LEFT:
Back of the centre-cupboard version showing drawers

BELOW RIGHT:
Version two, with false drawer front

SOME TIME AGO, in the middle of packing up my Yorkshire workshop to move to Shropshire, a client arrived unannounced to look at some of my display furniture which was for sale. I wasn't looking my best – army boots, khaki shorts, no shirt, no socks, and covered in a thick layer of dust! The workshop was a tip – with piles of timber and tools, and of course, more dust.

To his credit, the client was un-fazed and had a good look around. He did not find what he was after, but he really liked my office desk. He had been looking unsuccessfully for something similar for both his workplace and home – and so he commissioned me.

"I wasn't looking my best – army boots, khaki shorts, no shirt, no socks, and covered in a thick layer of dust!"

Commission

I was faced with quite a tall order – there were to be four large desks, two floor-to-ceiling glazed bookcases and sundry small cabinets; and this was a discerning client who wanted good, unusual timbers and quality work. I had no workshop, was moving house, and had some pretty serious commitments to make a kitchen and furniture for the new cottage – the buyer of our old cottage had bought a lot of the furniture which I had made.

My wife and I discussed it and

decided that we would need three months to set up in the new cottage, establish a workshop, and make our new bed! The client was pragmatic – if I could provide what he wanted he was prepared to wait, but we decided to go ahead to the design and costing stage before the move.

Design

Two of the desks were for the client, for both his office and home, one was for his PA, and one for his receptionist. I visited the factory and

"The client was pragmatic – if I could provide what he wanted he was prepared to wait"

the client's home to assess the situation, and in turn they all came to my workshop to talk over their requirements, and to look at various design features and samples of woods. They particularly liked the combination of burr elm and American walnut.

To allow for flexibility, all the desks were to have the same overall measurements. The top size was specified as 1625mm by 825mm (64in by 32in). This was too wide for drawers or cupboards on one side only if all the space was to be used – and from my observations at the factory office, that was necessary!

I suggested drawers at the back and cupboards in the front. The PA and the receptionist preferred a solid front to the knee space, while the client wanted his desk fronts open for more leg room. Various other features and requirements were specified and so I retired to the computer. The designs were drawn up, discussed with all the interested parties, modified, and finalised.

What emerged was two variations of essentially the same partner's desk. The only difference was that one had a solid front with a centre cupboard, and the other an open front with a false drawer. The requirement was for two of each variation.

Cutting out

The oak for the drawer casings and the burr for the door panels were marked out, cut, and dimensioned first. It was all placed in my workshop loft conditioner, out of the way, to settle. It would get maximum conditioning time whilst I was doing the main construction.

All thirty-plus cubes of the walnut were laid out, best-side up, against walls, on benches, on the floor, in the garage – wherever there was space. I started by selecting the largest and best-figured pieces for the tops. These were then cut a little oversize and stacked. The selection progressed down in size and visual importance until I was left with the trimmings to make some of the internal pieces, like drawer frames and shelves. There was little waste or spare. All this timber was now faced, thicknessed, and dimensioned to exact size.

LEFT: Kevin's own desk that inspired the client to make the commission

LEFT: Cramping the pedestal

TIMBER SELECTION

American walnut was chosen for the main desk carcasses, with contrasting burr elm fielded panels in the doors, and oak for the drawer casings.

The walnut gave the main part of the construction an inherent stability, which is an important factor in an office situation where the humidity level is likely to be even lower than in a centrally heated domestic environment.

The visual impact of the burr was maximised by placing it at the front, and the floating panels would be stabilised by being in the relatively broad-framed doors of walnut.

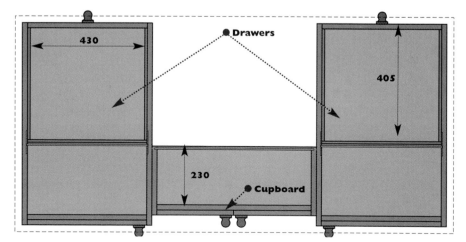

ABOVE: Pedestal side

Tops

The tops are made up first, each of four boards which are edge-matched to disguise the joint and get the best figure. The edges are machine-planed and finished by hand, to take out the planer ripples and leave the join length slightly hollow at the centre. This puts slight pressure on the ends and allows for any extra shrinkage of the end-grain. A slot, stopped 25mm (1in) short of the ends, is cut for a ply loose tongue which is fitted to strengthen the join. All are clamped and left to set, then finished down to 150 grit. They are sticked and stored flat with the top faces protected with hardboard sheet so that all other components can be stored on top of them.

The cramped and cluttered workshop, along with the fact that there were still many options and choices to make, meant that this was the most difficult, stressful, and potentially dangerous part of the operation. But it all seemed to go well, and it was with a great sense of relief that I stacked the finished pieces.

Sides

The 16-pedestal sides, of frame and panel construction, are tackled next. The bottom rail is deeper to take the moulded plinth, with the same depth showing above as the top rail. An insert is fitted to the inner face to house the back of the drawer frames and shelves. The inside edges of the frame are grooved 10mm by 10mm (⅜in by ⅜in) to take the panels, and the

corners are morticed and tenoned.

The panels are made of solid wood 10mm (⅜in) thick, deep sawn from 25mm (1in) boards, and edge-jointed, using the same technique as the tops, to the full size. The panel edges are left plain rather than fielded. The panel faces and the inside edges of the frames are finished, the sides assembled, checked for square and wind, and left to set.

The stopped housings to take the shelves and drawer frames are then cut with a router.

To do this, the sides are clearly marked as right and left handed, and all the cuts which can be made using the router fence, are done. A fixed fence is made from ply and batten, located at the top of the side for each of the remaining cuts.

Finally, the frames are finished to 150 grit, and stored.

Frames and shelves

The drawer frames are made up with a mortice and tenon at each corner and a ply lip glued and pinned along the outside edge, between it and the side panel, for the drawers to run against. The shelves are cut to size and finished at the same time.

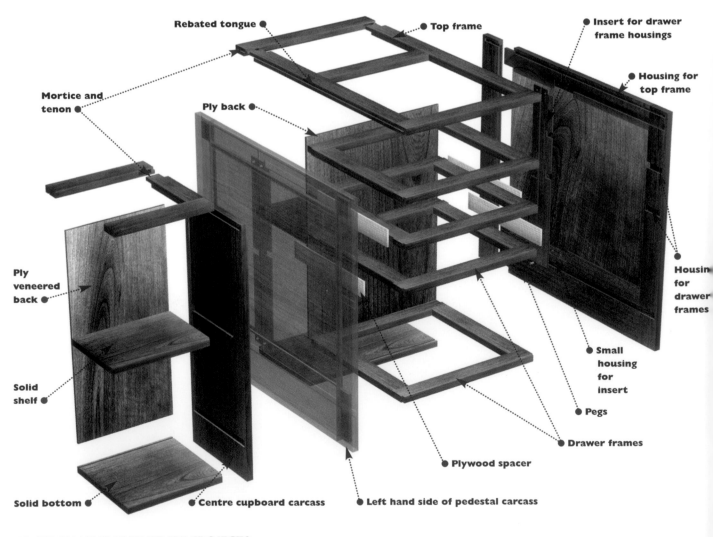

Rebated tongue ●

● Top frame

● Insert for drawer frame housings

Mortice and tenon ●

Ply back ●

● Housing for top frame

Ply veneered back ●

● Housing for drawer frames

Solid shelf ●

● Small housing for insert

● Pegs

● Drawer frames

Solid bottom ●

● Centre cupboard carcass

● Left hand side of pedestal carcass

● Plywood spacer

BATCH PRODUCTION

Although these desks were not designed specifically for a batch production run, the repeats of at least four of everything, and up to eighty of some items meant that some form of batch production would speed up the operation and keep the cost down.

Space
The first thing to look at was space – was there room to complete four of these desks in my small workshop? At first I thought that I would have to do two runs of two. Then I decided to make the major components, consisting of pedestals, tops, and centre cupboards/drawer fronts, and only completely assemble each desk in the workshop one at a time for tests and adjustments. They would then be dis-assembled, delivered as components, and I would assemble them all on site. It could be done as a straight run of four – just!

Organisation
The essence of batch production is care and organisation. Accurate cutting lists, careful sequencing of tasks, and use of rods and jigs for repeat measurements and tasks is essential.

I double-checked that I had the correct number, and sometimes a spare, of each item. Stacking up a pile to a known number, and then checking the number of stacks, helped. I became quite paranoid, wandering round the workshop counting little piles of wood and making chalk marks on them.

All the cuts, at a particular machine setting, were made at the same time, and the measurements of the first one-off

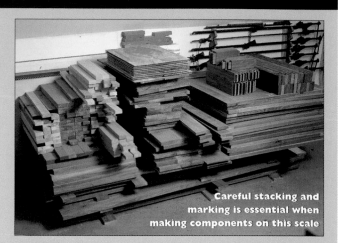
Careful stacking and marking is essential when making components on this scale

double-checked so that I didn't make eighty mistakes – it paid to make haste slowly.

Efficiency
The creative energy that would have been used to make four different desks, was channelled into making four similar pieces, efficiently. Perhaps some of the enjoyment of slower, progressive working was lost, but there was great satisfaction in the efficiency gained. I enjoyed the challenge – it appealed to someone with a military background!

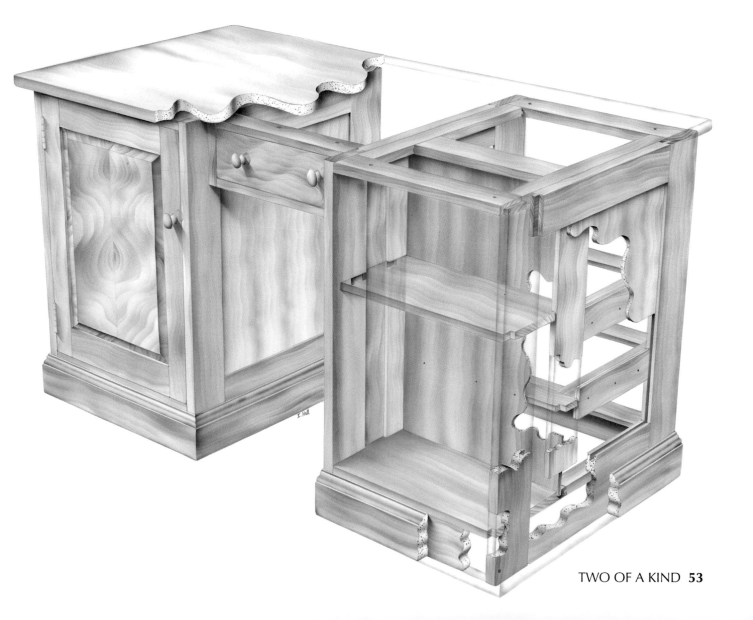

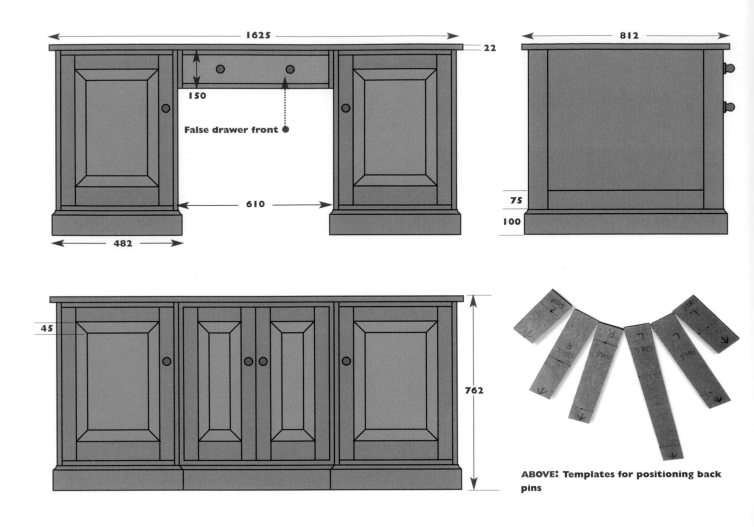

1625
22
150
False drawer front ●
610
482
812
75
100

45
762

ABOVE: Templates for positioning back pins

110.5
110.5
110.5
300

BELOW: Using hardboard jig for fixing the panel pins in the backs

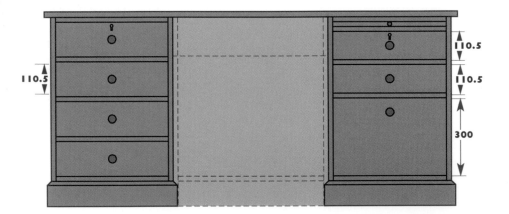

The frames and shelves are shouldered to fit the stopped housings in the side frames.

Burr door panels

The burr door panels are made up by deep-sawing the selected burr and match-jointing in the middle. This produces some ornamental effects in the figure and the colour. They are sticked and replaced in the conditioner until required. The partitions between the cupboard backs and the drawers are cut to size from 5mm (³⁄₁₆in) walnut-faced MDF.

At this stage I made sure I had done everything I could that required space in the workshop because the next phase was going to seriously eat into my floor area!

Pedestal assembly

All the pieces required for each pedestal are laid out and checked. The first is dry-fitted and then glued-up using Cascamite, clamped, checked for square, and left to set. I had sufficient clamps for two at a

time – the start-time was chalked on and the clamps left for at least four hours. While they were setting, the next two were being prepared, and before I knew it I was surrounded by pedestals.

The backs are pinned to the drawer frames and shelves using hardboard jigs which hold the pin in place for the hammer – a very simple but effective aid. ■

Home run

MAIN ILLUSTRATION BY IAN HALL

The second of the two-part project to make four partners' desks

HAVING COMPLETED the first stage in this small batch production of partners' desks, we are now ready to move into the final stages.

Plinths
The plinths are made from 16mm by 100mm (⅝in by 4in) pieces, with an ogee moulding cut on the top edge with a router. The pieces are cut to length and mitred on the radial arm saw, and adjusted by hand, where necessary, on a shooting board. I used a negative rake cross-cut saw which I was very pleased with in terms of finish and prevention of the blade 'climbing' over the work.

The plinths on the open-fronted desks are continuous all around the base of the pedestal. On the others, a gap is left on the inside to take the centre cupboards, with an internal mitred edge left at the front of the desk. The cupboards have a plinth at the front with mitred ends to slot in to the gap – this piece is made up at the same time.

At this point I got a biscuit jointer and, after a little experimentation and familiarisation, I used it on the plinth mitres. It was very useful in preventing them slipping when they were clamped up, quite apart from the obvious benefit of the extra strength.

The plinth is glued and screwed to the pedestal sides and a backing rail fitted between the sides at the front. Use a strap-clamp with blocks, and g-clamps, to get everything in position while the glue is wet, then screw through. The mitres are tapped over where necessary and sanded when dry. Titebond glue for dark woods will disguise any glue-line.

Centre cupboards
The centre cupboards are of simple construction. The sides are cut to size and a stopped housing is cut for the base and shelf. A slot is cut at the back of the sides to take a back of 5mm (³⁄₁₆in) MDF, faced on each side with walnut.

The base and shelf are cut to size and dry fitted. A backing rail for

> **"At this point I got a biscuit jointer and, after a little experimentation and familiarisation, I used it on the plinth mitres"**

PAPER REST
The paper rest is made from a frame of walnut, flush faced with walnut-faced MDF, and lipped with walnut edges. 25mm (1in) holes are drilled in the frame under the paper rest to give access for the screws fixing the top. The paper rests are fitted and a small pull attached. Stops to prevent the rest being pulled too far out are fitted from underneath once they are in position.

ABOVE: The challenge of batch production – but a more than satisfying result

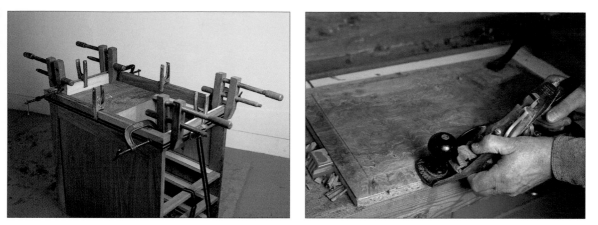

"The open-fronted desks have a false drawer front made of a 50mm by 19mm frame of walnut with a floating flush panel of burr to match the cupboard doors"

the plinth is made, to be fitted between the sides below the base, using biscuits.

All the pieces are then finished, glued, and clamped, checked for square, and left to set. The back is glued in all round for strength and the top biscuited flush down on to the sides. The pre-prepared plinth piece is then screwed and glued to the front.

False drawer fronts

The open-fronted desks have a false drawer front made of a 50mm by 19mm (2in by ¾in) frame of walnut with a floating flush panel of burr to match the cupboard doors. The burr panel is rebated, and let into a slot in the frame with a slight clearance gap at the edge, to look like a drawer – drawer pulls are also fitted.

This complete assembly is then screwed to the sides and top between the pedestals, from the inside rear.

Doors

Now that all the cupboards are made, check the front opening measurements and make the doors. All twelve are the same height with the four centre cupboard doors only

differing in width, which gives plenty of repeat cuts. The frames are made first – all the stiles and rails are dimensioned and the mortices and tenons cut. It is important with this number of repeats to get the mortices positioned correctly and the tenons exact, straight off the saw. The tenons' shoulders are cut on the radial arm saw, using the negative rake blade, and the cheeks are cut on the band-saw.

A slot is cut on the inside edges to take the fielded burr panels, and the inside edges of the frame's pieces are finished.

The burr panels are removed from the conditioner, cut to size, and fielded using a vertical profile cutter. Again, I found that there was plenty of use from each setting and the results were good, needing minimal hand-planing and sanding to finish the job.

The panel faces are finished and the doors assembled, glued and clamped, checked for square and wind, and left to set.

Fitting doors

Once set, the faces of the frames are finished, and the completed doors are matched, paired, and marked. Then

each one is fitted to its opening, leaving about 1mm (1⁄16in) clearance all round – this is finally adjusted to 2mm (3⁄32in) on final fitting.

The hinges are recessed into the frame only, and not the carcass side, which leaves a neater line. As they are all the same height, a simple jig can be made to position the hinge where it is scribed round with a scalpel. The router fence and depth can be set to take out the majority of the waste, and the recesses squared off with a sharp chisel.

DOOR AND DRAWER PULLS

I turned a batch of sixty or so pulls for all the doors and drawers. As I don't do a lot of turning I find it important to really standardise and repeat each action. I find the sizing tool from Craft Supplies invaluable and have at least two set to the relevant diameters to get them spot on. A piece of hardboard with the profile on one side, and the positions for marking the major cuts on the other, is also very helpful.

I always do extras for matching — and insurance. This leaves me with a box full of odd pulls which have been very useful over the years for pieces requiring only one or two.

**RIGHT: Marking
hinge positions
using hardboard
rod**

**FAR RIGHT:
Fitting a door
using a 2mm steel
rule for clearance**

The brass butt hinges are cleaned and
polished on the visible faces to take
out the machine marks, and screwed
into the recess. I send thanks to the
inventor of the Axminster self-centring
hinge pilot drill – a terrific buy at a
couple of quid – and, of course, my
power screwdriver.

Another simple hardboard jig can be
made to mark the approximate height
of the hinges on the inside face of the
cupboard, and a cutting gauge can be
used to scribe the screw line. The
doors are held at the correct height by
a metal rule wedged as a spacer
underneath them.

The screw line is centred in the
hinge screw hole and the self-centring

DRAWERS

Cutting dovetails
on the bandsaw

Using lock upside down
to mark its socket

All the pieces for the drawers are cut to size, fitted
and marked. The fronts are made from 22mm
(⅞in) walnut, the carcasses from 10mm (⅜in) oak,
and the bases from 5mm (³⁄₁₆in) oak-faced MDF.
The sides are slotted for the bases, taped together
in double pairs with the top one marked out, and
the pins cut on the bandsaw.

The fronts and backs are marked one at a time
from the pins, and the majority of the waste
removed with a router. Each joint is then
individually finished with a sharp chisel. The drawer
is then assembled, with the MDF base glued in all
round and pinned at the back, checked for square
and wind, and left to set.

Before assembling the top drawers, the locks are
fitted to the fronts, for ease of working – the locks
are positioned and the hole for the key

pin-marked in the centre of the drawer at the
correct height and drilled through. The key-hole in
my locks was not central so that the lock body was
offset. The locks are marked upside down, the recess
routed out leaving a shallow shoulder for the screws,
then finished by hand, and fitted.

The escutcheon is positioned over the pilot
hole, and tapped smartly with a small hammer, to
leave an imprint on the wood. The keyhole is cut
to this imprint with a chisel, a thin touch of
Araldite is applied to the hole, and the escutcheon
is tapped home.

The drawers are then fitted and clearly marked on
the back to identify their position and which desk
they belong to. Bright steel supports, 16mm by 3mm
(⅝ by ⅛in), are fitted to the deep file drawers to
carry suspended files.

The escutcheon is tapped to leave imprint to cut to

File drawer open,
showing supports

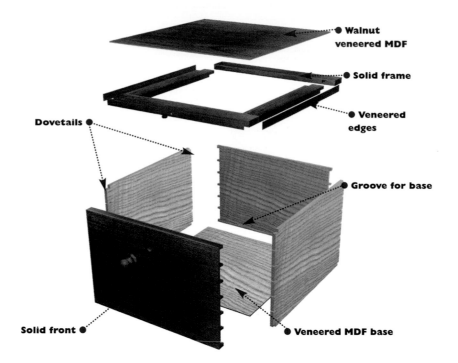

Walnut veneered MDF

Solid frame

Veneered edges

Dovetails

Groove for base

Solid front

Veneered MDF base

pilot drill used to drill one pilot hole in each hinge. The screw is driven home and the door checked for fit, adjustments are made, the remaining holes drilled, and the screws are driven in.

Brass double ball catches are fitted to the doors – which is easier on the pedestals that have no tops – you can get your hand in to hold them in position. Not so on the centre cupboards – they have to be carefully measured. The spring loading on the balls is adjusted to get a satisfying 'clunk'.

Trial assembly
At this point the desks are trial-assembled, one at a time, on a level platform on the floor of the workshop – use a piece of 2438mm by 1219mm by 25mm (8ft by 4ft by 1in) MDF checked flat and levelled with wedges. All final tests and adjustments can now be made.

The tops are attached using screws through slots in the top rails of the pedestals. The centre cupboards and false drawer fronts are screwed through from the inside to the pedestal side frames. A fillet on the back edge of the centre cupboards

fills the gap between the frame and the panel.

Finish
I chose a danish oil finish to really enhance the walnut and burr elm – and its renewability would be useful in an office environment.

Carefully check for glue marks and finally hand sand everything down to 320 grit. Then apply a

liberally first coat of oil, and renew it every hour or so for a day, until the wood will take no more. The porous burr takes a lot more than the close-grained walnut. Remove all surplus oil, to prevent any build up on the surface, and leave it to dry and harden, in a warm dry workshop, for 24 hours.

This surface is cut back by hand with 320 grit, followed by a

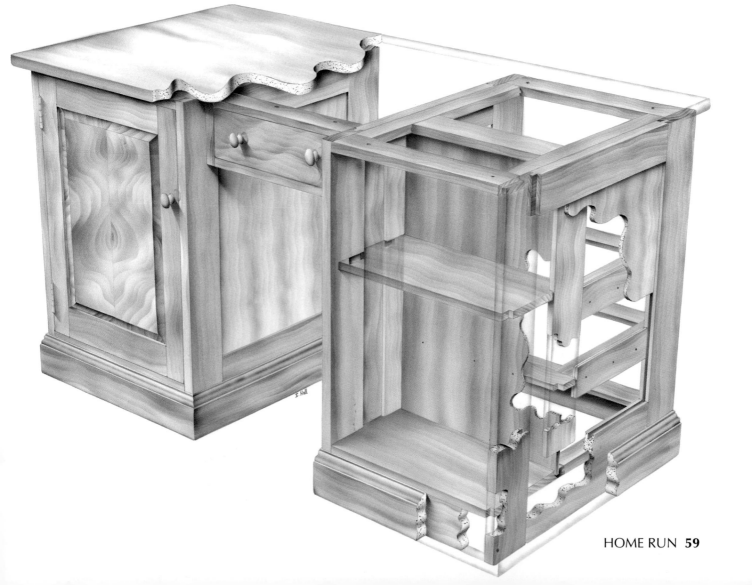

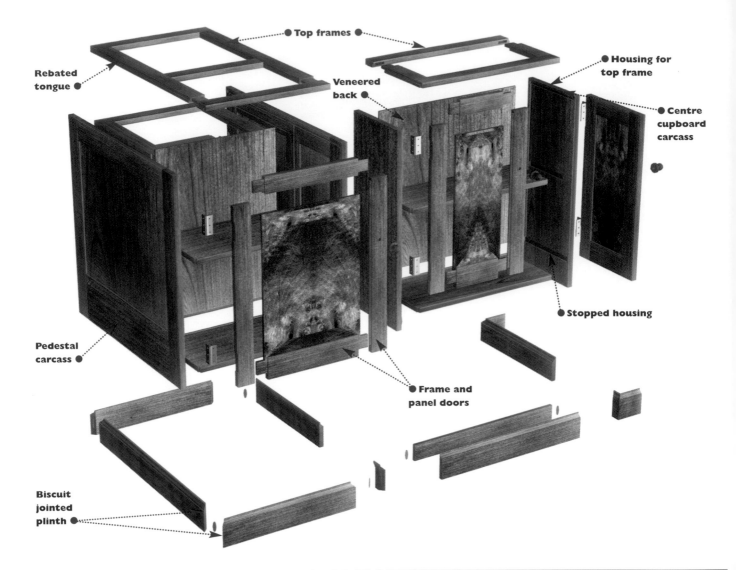

Rebated
tongue

Top frames

Housing for
top frame

Veneered
back

Centre
cupboard
carcass

Pedestal
carcass

Stopped housing

Frame and
panel doors

Biscuit
jointed
plinth

DELIVERY AND ASSEMBLY

Arrangements were made for the desks to be delivered as components, as a part load on a furniture van from my usual haulier.
I went up to lovely Teesdale to assemble them on site.

I hate working away from my workshop and always leave something behind, but on this occasion all went well, though it took
a good bit longer than I thought it would. The desks were positioned, assembled, minor adjustments made where necessary,
and wiped over with a very thin coat of teak oil to show them off.

All the components were made so that they could be assembled on site

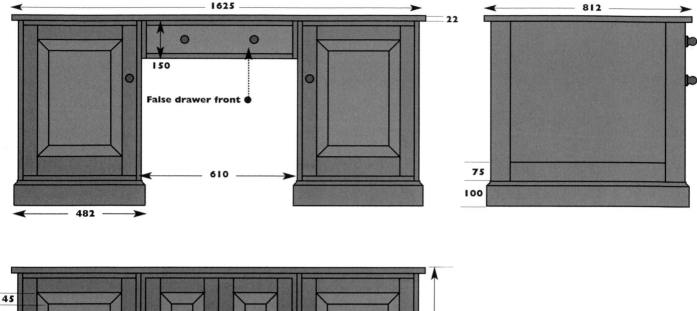

1625
22
150
False drawer front
610
482
812
75
100

45
762

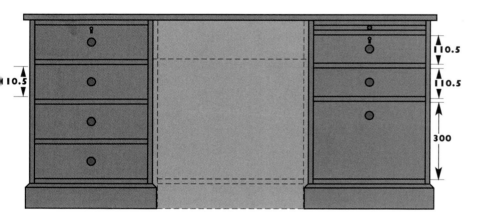

110.5
110.5
10.5
10.5
300

"It was challenging, very satisfying, and enjoyable – in a different way to the normal run of things"

light coat of oil every 24 hours for a week, cutting back between coats with a Scotchbrite grey pad. Then allow ten days for final hardening. Just before delivery, apply a thin coat of teak oil. I supply the client with a bottle of this same oil and a Scotchbrite grey pad for their future use.

Incidentally, I have produced a leaflet on the care and use of solid wood furniture which I give to all my clients now. General knowledge, in these days of central heating and stable MDF and veneers, cannot be relied on – believe me!

Conclusion

This was a major task at the wrong time, but I was glad that I took it on. It was challenging, very satisfying, and enjoyable in a different way to the normal run of things. The end result pleased the client and his staff, and the desks, being in public view, have received much favourable comment – never a bad thing! ■

SUPPLIERS

Axminster Power Tools Centre – 0800 371822
Titebond glue for dark woods
Self-centring hinge pilot drill

Wealdon Cutters – 0800 3284183
Negative rake crosscut blade
Vertical profile cutter

Craft Supplies – 0800 146417
Sizing tool

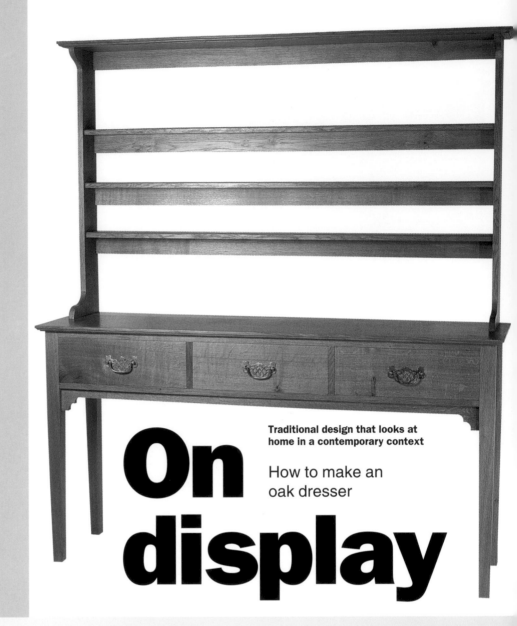

Traditional design that looks at home in a contemporary context

On display

How to make an oak dresser

"I liked the overall concept and kept a mental note – and when a client approached me to build a display dresser for a dining room, it was a good starting point"

ome time ago, when visiting Raby Castle in Co. Durham, I saw in the kitchens a large, old, oak dresser with about a 2133mm (7ft) span to the shelves. Even though it was so big it still looked relatively delicate having a table base and no back to the top unit. However, the shelves had not been braced properly and had, over the years, sagged badly in the middle.

Nevertheless, I liked the overall concept and kept a mental note – and when a client approached me to build a display dresser for a dining room, it was a good starting point.

Design

The client needed plenty of display shelf space for china, and storage for cutlery – and wanted the dresser not to project too far into the room, nor look too heavy and imposing. It was to have a table base with drawers under and a display top with narrow, grooved shelves

on which to display the china. Remembering the fate of the Raby dresser shelves, I included rails under them to brace the shelf above and give the china on the shelf below a support to rest against.

Timber selection

I visited the client's home to look at the dining room; the existing furniture was all in English oak and of a nice simple, country style. The dresser was to be in a complementary style and also of English oak. We decided on the final measurements, and I retired to draw up the piece on the computer, using Autosketch.

Timber preparation

Once the design and measurements had been finalised I set off to my usual timber merchants where I managed to get some nicely figured, quarter-sawn English oak from their excellent stocks.

Back in the workshop the wood was laid out, marked up, and cut oversize to allow for final trimming. The best figured pieces were chosen for the drawer fronts, and the top of the base unit.

It was then faced and thicknessed, checked for faults, figure, and colour, and marked. Next it was sticked, stacked, and placed in the conditioning cabinet to settle and adjust. Two weeks later it was brought into the workshop and dimensioned to final sizes.

Base unit construction

Top

The selected pieces for the top are arranged, best face up, in the most pleasing figure pattern, with the figure as far as possible running through the joint lines to disguise them. The adjoining

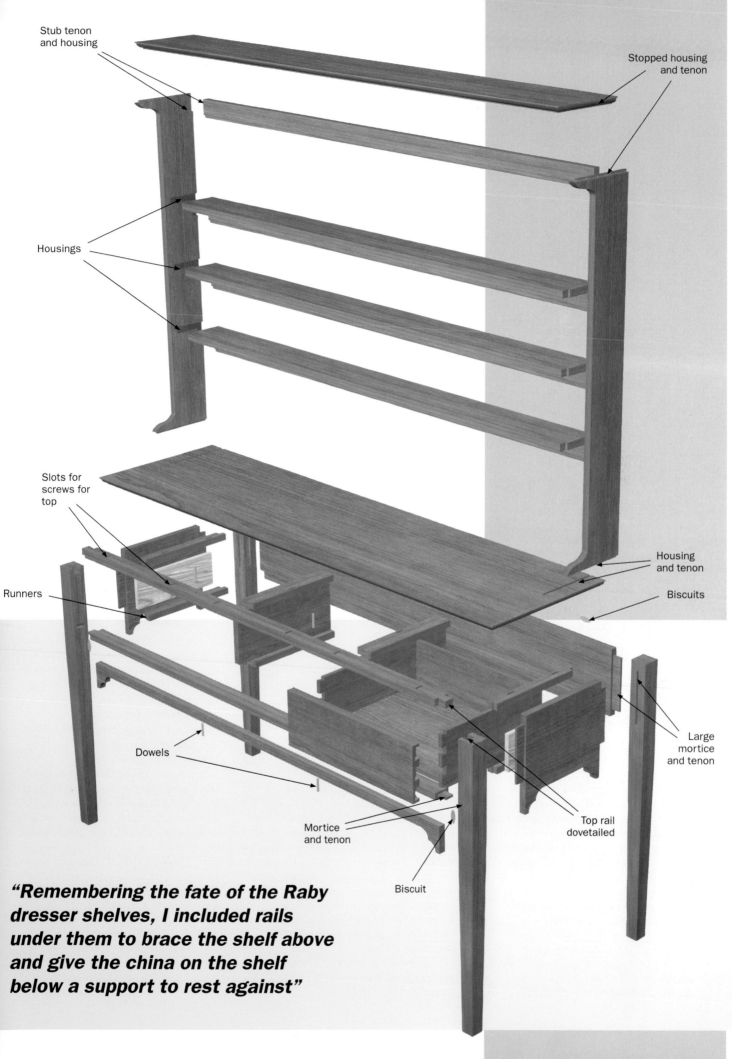

Stub tenon
and housing

Stopped housing
and tenon

Housings

Slots for
screws for
top

Housing
and tenon

Biscuits

Runners

Large
mortice
and tenon

Dowels

Top rail
dovetailed

Mortice
and tenon

Biscuit

*"Remembering the fate of the Raby
dresser shelves, I included rails
under them to brace the shelf above
and give the china on the shelf
below a support to rest against"*

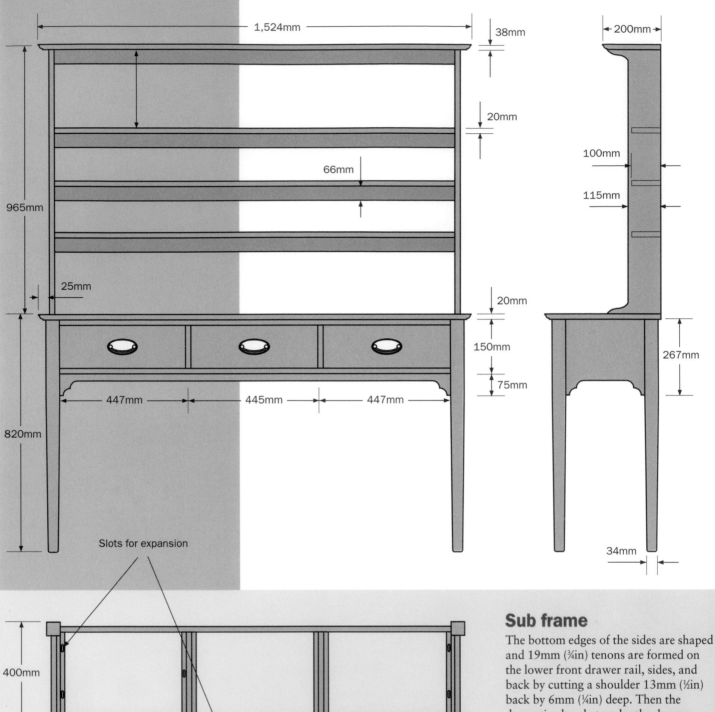

Slots for expansion

Sub frame

The bottom edges of the sides are shaped and 19mm (¾in) tenons are formed on the lower front drawer rail, sides, and back by cutting a shoulder 13mm (½in) back by 6mm (¼in) deep. Then the decorative bracket under the drawer bottom rail is cut to shape on the jigsaw and bandsaw, finished, and fitted into position with dry biscuits.

The front rail over the drawer tops is dovetailed into the tops of the legs, and the cross rails above and below the drawers fitted, with biscuits, to the front rails and the back. The joints are tested dry to check the fit, then the whole carcass assembly is put together dry, and disassembled.

All the pieces are finished to 150 grit, and the front and back glued up and assembled, checked for square and left to set. Once they have set, the sides and top and bottom drawer cross rails are fitted – the whole subframe is checked for square in all directions, and again left to set.

The uprights between the drawers are

edges are machine-planed first, then hand-planed to remove the ripples, and the middles slightly hollowed so that the ends pull up tight when they are clamped. Biscuits are used to reinforce the joins, glue is applied, and the top clamped and left to set.

The front and side edges are then shaped with a router, using an ovolo cutter, and sanded to a finish.

Legs

The legs are morticed for the sides, back, and the front bottom rail, under the drawers. The biscuit slots for the

decorative bracket under that rail are also cut, before tapering.

The taper begins 280mm (11in) down from the top of the leg, and can be achieved in a number of different ways – with jigs, on the planer, thicknesser, or circular saw – but I found the simplest, safest, and most enjoyable method was to rough them out on the bandsaw and finish by hand. Oak is such a joy to work with a sharp, well set, plane – and the exercise is good for you!

The feet of the legs are rounded over to prevent splintering or catching on a carpet.

Base, showing shaping on bottom rail

Fittings

To match other fittings in the room we consulted H E Savill's excellent Period Cabinet Fittings catalogue and selected some handles with a nicely-shaped cut-out back plate. These are positioned and the fixing holes drilled in the drawer fronts before finishing the dresser, but the handles are only fitted after all the finishing is complete.

H E Savill Period Cabinet Fittings tel: 01723 373032.

Word of warning

Wire wool should never be used to rub oak down as the acid in the wood will eat any minute particles of it that have snagged in the grain, and leave small black marks. For the same reason I used zinc-coated screws and brass fittings. Iron or steel, nails, screws, or fittings are not suitable for oak.

"Oak is such a joy to work with a sharp, well set, plane – and the exercise is good for you!"

doweled into position through the top and bottom front drawer rails. Spacers are glued and pinned to the sides and to the drawer cross rails for the drawers to run against.

Fitting top

As the shelf unit would be fitted to the back of this top I decided to fix it at the back to the subframe and allow for the inevitable movement at the front only. I felt this would give more stability to the shelf unit above – full of expensive china!

Slots are cut in the drawer top cross rails and the front rail before assembly of the sub frame. They are countersunk on the underside to take zinc-plated screws which hold the top flat and allow for movement across the grain, from back to front. The back is fixed with biscuits through the underside of the top into the top edge of the back. This hopefully ensures that relatively little movement will take place at the back – the movement would be in the overhang at the front which would adjust to cope.

Drawer detail

Finishing

The existing oak furniture is a very nice honey colour and I wanted the dresser to match it. It would darken slightly with time and exposure to light, of course, so it was important that it should be finished a bit lighter than the existing furniture now, and allowed to catch up.

The whole piece is checked for glue marks and imperfections, then finally hand-sanded with 240 grit followed by 320 grit.

Two light coats of linseed oil diluted with one-third white spirit are applied and each coat allowed to dry for 48 hours in my warm, dry workshop. A light coat of Danish oil is then applied to harden and seal the finish. All is left for about ten days before a light rub down with a Scotchbrite grey pad – a final finishing of two coats of clear wax are applied and buffed to a sheen.

Cutlery tray

"As the shelf unit would be fitted to the back of this top I decided to fix it at the back to the subframe and allow for the inevitable movement at the front only"

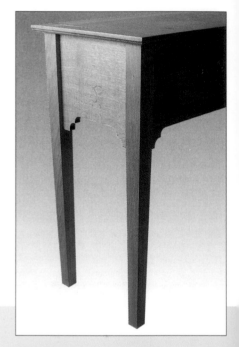

Side view

Drawers

The drawer fronts and casings are cut to size. The fronts are made from 22mm (⅞in) and the remainder of the casings from 10mm (⅜in) oak. The bases are from oak-faced MDF glued in all round to add strength. The tails are cut out under-size on the bandsaw and finished to size with a paring chisel. The majority of the waste for the pins is removed with a router and again they are finished with a sharp paring chisel. The drawers are then assembled and fitted in the usual way.

Cutlery inserts

Two of the drawers have removable cutlery trays resting on rails which are glued and screwed to the insides of the drawers. They are a simple, sectioned, box construction using off-cuts and size 0 biscuits. Measurements are for the specific cutlery set. They made best use of the storage in the drawers and would be useful when setting the table.

Shelf unit

Sides

The 19mm (¾in) wide by 6mm (¼in) deep stopped housings for the shelves and the support rails are cut in the sides and the tops and bottoms shouldered, before shaping them on the bandsaw.

Shelves

A groove is cut in the top face of each of the shelves to locate the display china. The shelves and support rails are shouldered to fit in to the stopped housings in the sides, and checked to fit. The shelves and sides are then finished to 150 grit, assembled using Titebond, clamped, checked square, and left to set.

Top

A single piece of oak is used for the top with the best face downwards, and the edges shaped with the same ovolo cutter used on the top of the base unit. Stopped housings for the sides are cut in the underside of this top and the top side of the base unit. The top of the shelf unit is finished and glued into position.

The whole shelf unit is then offered up to the base unit with the bottom of the side locating, dry, into the stopped housings cut in the top of the base unit. A 50mm (2in) zinc-plated screw is countersunk, at an angle, through the back of each side, at an angle, into the base unit top, to secure the shelf unit and prevent any forward movement.

Conclusion

The client was pleased with the piece and it looked just right in its final setting. I enjoyed making it and it underlined to me the value of seeing lots of different furniture and learning from one's observations. ∎

Coffee table blend

Rosewood reflects Mackintosh in this table which makes prudent use of salvaged elm and off-cuts

THE MIX OF ELM (*Ulmus procera*) and rosewood (*Dalbergia sp*) from which this table is made is the result of an unlikely-sounding but true background story.

A tree in our bottom field fell victim to Dutch Elm Disease; it had to come down, but I managed to salvage the main trunk, having it cut into through and through boards which were air-dried for several years.

To make up for losing the elm from our view, I decided to make furniture for our house from its timber, and that's where the rosewood comes in.

While in Belize, an RAF friend of mine stumbled across a thirsty American gentleman holding a licence to take out two rosewood trees. A deal was done and a quantity of NAAFI beer was exchanged for off-cuts subsequently brought back to the UK.

I got to keep the off-cuts of the off-cuts!

"It would be subjected to fairly heavy routine use as a resting place for cups, drinks and feet"

Design

I must confess to having visited Hill House in Glasgow – designed and furnished by Charles Rennie Mackintosh – just before I designed this piece.

A great admirer of Mackintosh's designs, I tried to include something of his influence. He often used decorative square cut-outs, and my design reflects this with contrasting square inserts and panels of rosewood within the elm.

The colours blend effectively and the design maximises the effect of the rosewood, while using only a small amount of this rare and expensive timber.

The table was going into a large sitting room walled with rough stone and with a heavy-beamed ceiling and earth-coloured soft furnishings.

It would sit in the centre of a square Persian-pattern rug, and would be subjected to fairly heavy routine use as a resting place for cups, drinks and feet. A magazine shelf was also required, so I added more interest by placing an inlay on it; I like there to be more to see after the first impression.

The design developed into the desired effect – a robust, but not too agricultural-looking table in warm-coloured woods.

The colours of the elm and rosewood complement the decor of the room, and the structure of the table suits its general look.

Timber selection

The 38mm (1½in) elm boards easily dressed down to 28mm (1⅛in) – although quite a lot of it had been attacked by wood-boring insects and had to be cut out and burned. From what was left I carefully selected the figure of the top boards to achieve the most pleasing pattern.

All the pieces of wood were cut oversize and then conditioned in my kiln for a month.

The available rosewood was from two different trees, the wood from one being quite brown and from the other my desired deep purple, *see panel*. This too was selected, cut oversize and conditioned with the elm.

Because I was after the colour effect, I chose wood with very plain figuring for these small pieces.

"I don't normally alternate the cupping direction of tangentially sawn boards, finding that this only produces a ripple effect"

THE COLOUR PURPLE

The rosewood which Kevin Ley acquired is most likely to be Honduras rosewood (*Dalbergia stevensonii*). This particular tree reaches its best development in the coastal region of British Honduras – now Belize – according to the invaluable *An Encyclopedia of World Timbers* by Titmuss, our copy published by The Technical Press in 1959.

Unlike its Brazilian rosewood (*Dalbergia nigra*) cousin, which has heartwood ranging from chocolate to very deep brown, the Honduran variety varies from dull brown to almost purple, thus explaining the two different colours in Ley's possession.

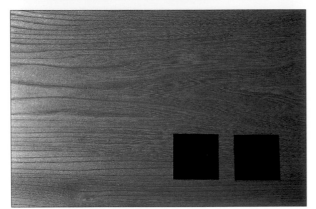

TOP: Scribing the rosewood with a scalpel held at an angle to mark out for inlaying the top

ABOVE: The finished result

Top, shelf

The selected top and shelf boards were, unfortunately, all tangentially sawn, but I felt that the side frames gave plenty of scope to lock the top down to prevent cupping. The shelf, being tenoned in along its entire width, has the same effect.

I don't normally alternate the cupping direction of tangentially sawn boards, finding that this only produces a ripple effect; at least if they are all trying to cup in the same direction they can be braced flat more easily!

The boards are matched for the most pleasing figure and the joining edges planed. The fit of the joining edges is slightly concave, touching at each end with a 0.8mm (¹⁄₃₂in) gap at the centre. This helps to pull the clamps up tight, and allows for extra shrinkage at the ends when drying out.

To add strength, the joining edges are then slotted for a loose tongue, the slots being stopped 25mm (1in) short of the ends so that the tongue is unseen.

After checking for flatness, PVA glue is applied to the edges, and the top and shelf clamped up and left to set.

> "To undercut the inlays slightly, I marked around them with a scalpel held at an angle"

Inlays

The inlays on the top are 50mm (2in) square and 6mm (¼in) thick. To undercut them slightly, I marked around them with a scalpel held at an angle, *see photo*. To aid this operation, the sides of the inlays are very slightly tapered towards the base.

The majority of the recess waste is removed with a router, set to just under 6mm (¼in) depth, leaving the inlay just proud of the surface when fitted. The recess is cut accurately to the edge with a 25mm (1in) chisel, locating it in the scored mark left by the scalpel.

Checking the fit of the inlay in the recess, and adjusting the taper of the sides, helps their location and provides an easy start to driving them home – the hardness of the rosewood also compresses the elm to produce a tight fit.

To avoid a glue line, PVA is applied just below the top edge of the recesses; a wooden block is placed over the inlays before they are driven home with a mallet.

Once set, they are levelled to the top with a fine-set, sharp smoothing plane. The 100mm (4in) square inlay in the centre of the shelf is fitted in the same way.

Side frame

The grain in the side frame runs from top to bottom, in the same direction as the grain in the table top to which it is tenoned. This allows the sides and top to move in the same direction and by the same amount.

While moisture level changes will result in the overall size of the table changing slightly, the structure should not be affected.

Each outside piece of the side

LEFT: Side view showing rosewood panels – note the direction of grain in relation to the top

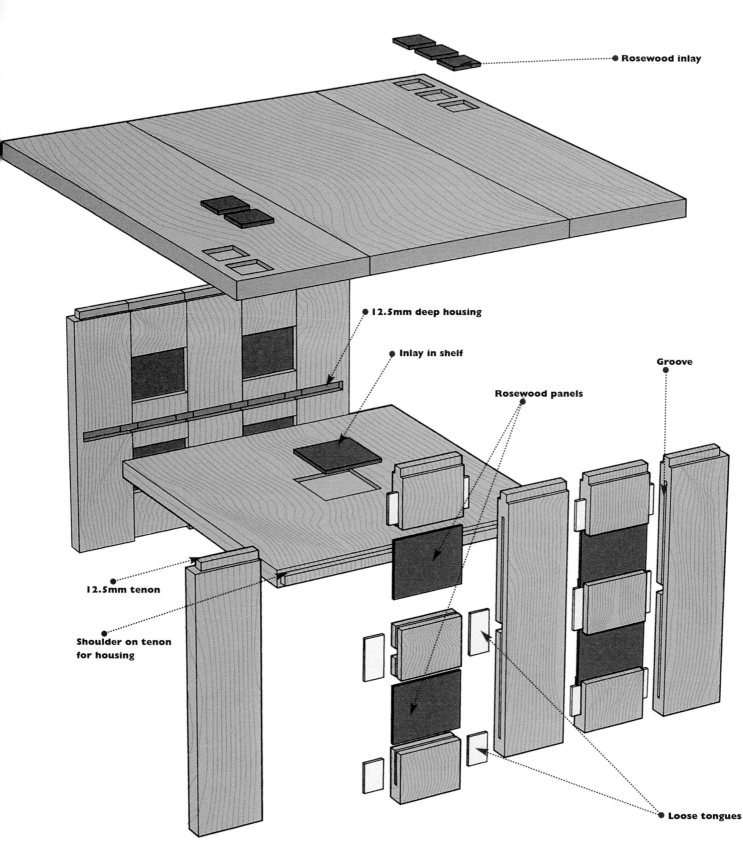

Rosewood inlay

12.5mm deep housing

Inlay in shelf

Rosewood panels

Groove

12.5mm tenon

Shoulder on tenon for housing

Loose tongues

frame is joined to the centre
piece with three short lengths,
separated to leave the cut-outs
for the panels. The short lengths
are spaced to allow the bottom
one to be 6mm (¼in) clear of
the ground, forming three feet,
see diagram.

Panels to take the housings are
cut 6mm wide by 6mm deep
(¼ by ¼in), around the cut-out
edges. Again, the edge joints are
slotted to take loose tongues.

Panels
The panels are cut to size, and
finished. Left plain rather than
being fielded, they are fitted
6mm (¼in) into the side frames.

The side frames are dry-fitted
with the panels in place, and
adjustments made. PVA glue is
applied to the frame edge joints,
but not, of course, to the panels.
The side frames are clamped,
checked for square and flatness,
and left to set.

Assembly
A 16mm (⅝in) wide by 13mm
(½in) deep housing is cut in the
sides to take the shelf, leaving a
6mm (¼in) shoulder at each end.
The tenon on the shelf is formed
with a router, and 6mm (¼in)
shoulders cut with a tenon saw.

The shelf is assembled dry and
adjusted to fit.

A similar housing cut in the
underside of the top takes the
upper edges of the side frames;

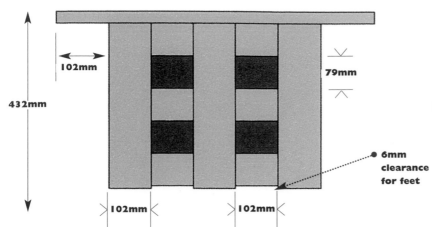

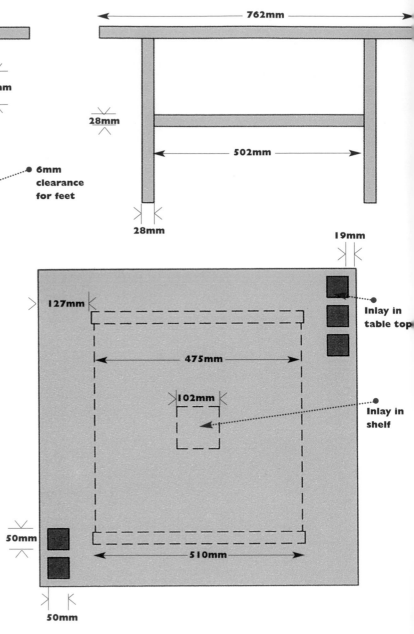

ABOVE AND RIGHT: Front, side and top elevations

BELOW: Oiling the table

tenons are formed on the top edges of the side frames, and shouldered in the same way as on the shelf. The joints are assembled dry to check the fit.

The shelf and the inside faces of the sides are sanded and finished. To ensure that the tenon drives the glue in to the joint, PVA glue is applied to the top edges all around the housing, and clamps applied. It is checked for square and left to set.

When set, the outside edges of the sides and the underside of the top are finally sanded and finished. Glue is applied to the top of the housing and the sides clamped to it.

After checking for square in all directions, the piece is left to set before finishing, *see panel.*

Conclusion

I made several pieces of furniture from my old elm, and this table is, after several years, still giving good service.

It seems fitting to me that the tree lives on as a piece of furniture, still appreciated but in a different way. ■

CUTTING BACK AND HARDENING

To accord with the fairly robust use for which this table is designed, I chose a danish oil finish – not so much because it is tough but more because it is renewable!

After carefully checking for glue marks, I hand-sand everything down to 320 grit.

Then I follow my normal practice of a liberally applied first coat of oil, renewed every hour or so for a day, until the wood really will take no more.

At this point I remove all surplus oil, to prevent any build up on the surface, and leave it to harden in a warm, dry place for 24 hours.

This surface is then cut back by hand with 320 grit, followed by a light coat of oil every 24 hours for a week, cutting back between coats with a Scotchbrite grey pad. I allow ten days for final

hardening before putting the table to good use.

The surface has been renewed several times since it was finished by cutting the surface right back with a Scotchbrite grey pad, and applying a further light coat of danish oil.

This method works well as long as the surface is well cut back to ensure no build up of oil.

To give the new coat plenty of time to harden before use, I usually do this just before we are going away for a few days.

Minor improvement between renewals can be made with a very light coat of linseed or teak oil. Cutting back with the grey pad before each application of oil prevents a 'syrupy' look developing – and often the grey pad treatment is enough with no further oil of any sort.

Making contrasts

How to make a fumed oak and sycamore side table

MADE THIS side table to complement the corner cupboard and seven-drawer chest – also in fumed oak and sycamore – that are also featured in this book. They are all in my study and serve both as display pieces and useful articles of furniture – the side table holds my collection of magazines for easy reference!

Design
As usual when making furniture for our own use I try to incorporate something new, unusual, difficult, or experimental – for me! So I put the tenon for the front and back stretchers on the curve of the leg, instead of the much easier straight part, made the top out of a mixture of fumed and un-fumed wood, and put contrasting inlays on the front and back top frame.

I drew it up several times, and, once I was sure I wasn't just being bloody minded and the table looked right, I decided to go ahead.

Timber selection
The oak and sycamore was selected from the same batch as the seven-drawer chest, with the exception of the thicker stuff for the legs which came from some 38mm (1½in) French oak left from a previous job. All the timber was cut oversize and put in my conditioning cabinet for three weeks – the top, in particular, would need some final conditioning at a later stage.

Top
The top is made up from three pieces of sycamore, and two of oak, which are later fumed. As no adjustments can be made after fuming the oak,

the top is made up and finished dry, using loose tongues – or biscuits – and clamps to locate the pieces. The top edges are rounded over to a 6mm (¼in) radius. Still dry and in the clamps, the top is finally sanded and placed in room temperature to adjust to the conditions.

Legs
The oak for the legs is faced and thicknessed to 31mm (1¼in), a hardboard template is made of the shape of the leg, and the legs marked out. They are then cut out carefully on the band-saw and finished with a plane, spokeshave, and scraper.

The mortices are cut 13mm (½in) deep for the top frame, as are the mortices for the side stretchers. The mortices for the front and back stretchers are cut 19mm (¾in) deep at the top to allow for the loss of depth

ABOVE LEFT:
Using contrasting timbers can make for some interesting variations

DECORATION

ABOVE: Close-up of the inlay details

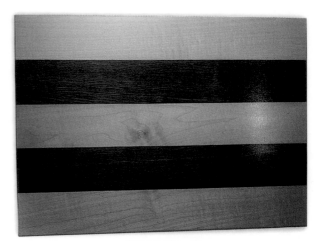

ABOVE: The top

The inlays are made from 6mm (¼in) thick oak and fumed overnight in a biscuit tin after all adjustments have been made. This means that the front face cannot be planed to get a flush fit – only the lightest sanding is feasible.

Mark around the diamond shapes with a scalpel, held at an angle, to slightly under-cut them. The sides of the inlays are very slightly tapered towards the base to help with this under-cutting.

The majority of the recess waste for the diamond shapes can be removed with a router set to exactly the inlay thickness so that the inlay is flush with the surface when fitted. The recess is chiselled out accurately to the edge, locating the chisel in the scored mark left by the scalpel.

The line inlay recesses are cut with the router using a 6mm (¼in) straight cutter and the inlay pieces rounded at the ends with a sanding block.

The fit of all the inlays should be checked on the recesses and the taper of the sides adjusted, where necessary, to help them to locate and give an easy start to driving them home. I left them a fraction oversize as the oak, being harder, would compress the sycamore to give a tight fit.

PVA glue is applied just below the top edge of the recesses – to avoid a glue line, a wooden block is placed over the inlays, then they are driven home with a mallet, flush to the surface, and left to set. Once set, they are lightly sanded flush where necessary.

ABOVE: Marking inlay with a scalpel

in the curve, *see main diagram*. To do this, I used the fence of the morticer on my planer on the straight part of the leg as a reference.

The underside edges of the foot of the legs are rounded over to a 6mm (¼in) radius to prevent break-out, and allow easy sliding on a carpet. The legs and two centre pieces of the top are then put through a process called fuming. After fuming, the two centre pieces of the top are replaced in the clamps, in room temperature.

BELOW: Fig 1 Marking the curve

Stretchers

The sycamore for the stretchers are faced and thicknessed to 16mm (⅝in) and the side stretchers are cut to length and width. Straightforward tenons are cut 13mm (½in) long to fit the mortices on the legs.

The front and rear stretchers are cut to size, allowing the extra length for the curve of the legs. The tenons were initially cut 13mm (½in) deep and offered up to the mortices in the legs. They fitted at the top but not at the bottom, of course, because of the curve

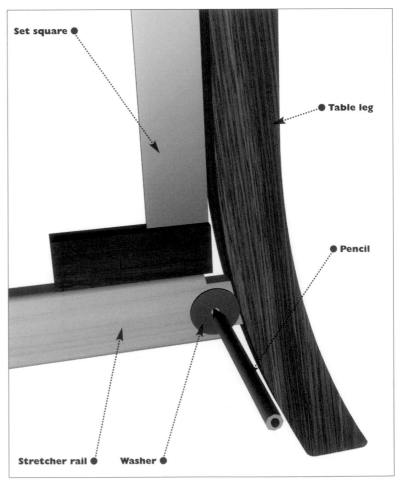

Set square ●

● Table leg

● Pencil

Stretcher rail ●   Washer ●

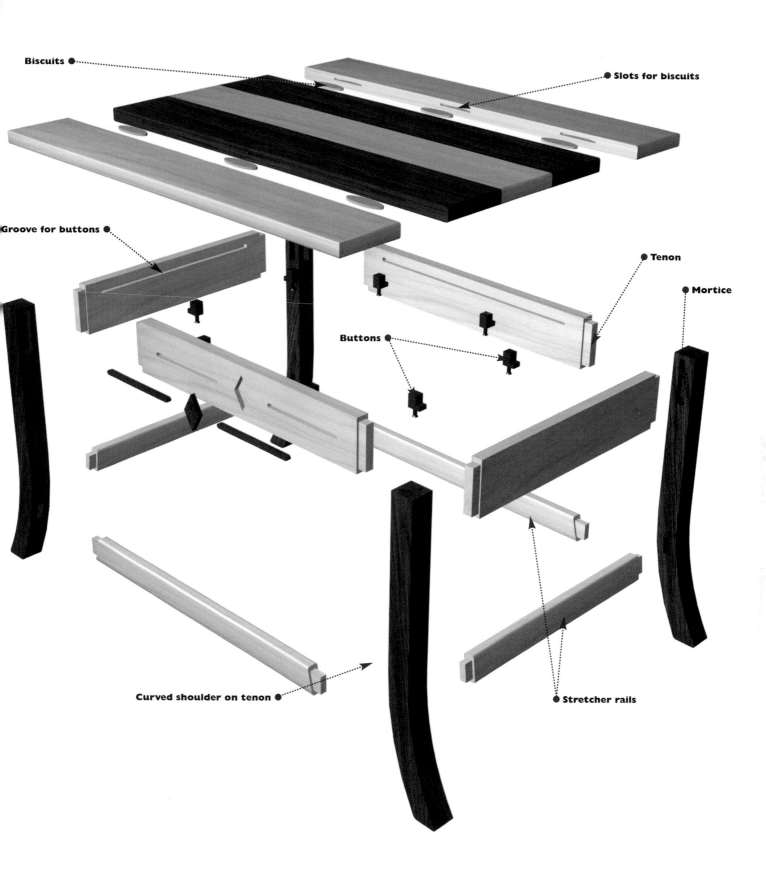

Biscuits ●

Slots for biscuits ●

Groove for buttons ●

Tenon ●

● **Mortice**

Buttons ●

Curved shoulder on tenon ●

● **Stretcher rails**

of the leg. Setting the stretcher square to the leg, I used a pencil in a suitably sized washer to trace the curve of the leg on to the shoulder of the tenon, *see Fig 1*. The shoulders were then finished to the line with a paring chisel, the tenons completed, and checked for fit.

The top and bottom edges of all the stretchers are rounded over to a 6mm (¼in) radius, to soften them.

Top frame

The top frame pieces are faced and thicknessed to 19mm (¾in) and cut to length and width. 13mm (½in) tenons are cut on the ends to fit the mortices at the top of the legs. A 6mm by 6mm (¼in by ¼in) slot 13mm (½in) down from the top edge is cut in all four pieces to take the buttons which will be used

to fix the top.

The buttons are made of scraps of oak and sycamore – when fitted, the top of the button is slightly below the top of the frame so that the top can be pulled down on to it by the screws.

Holes are drilled in the button using a combined tapered drill and countersink.

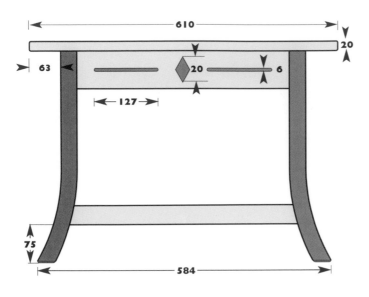

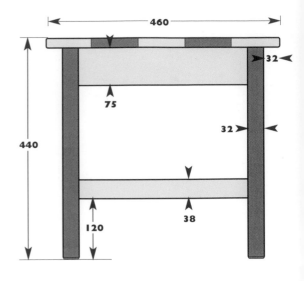

Assembly

The top is glued-up, checking all the levels, joints and edges carefully, making adjustments only to the sycamore. It is then left to set.

The front and back top frame pieces and the front and back stretchers are fitted to the legs, glued, clamped, checked for square, and left to set.

The sides of the top frame and side stretchers are then glued and clamped, forming the pedestal. This should be checked for square and level and left to set. I have a 1220mm by 1220mm (4ft by 4ft) piece of MDF on the floor of my workshop, which is flat and set level,

for standing such pieces on while they set true – hopefully!

The top is then fitted using the buttons to allow for the inevitable future movement.

Finishing

The whole piece should be checked carefully for glue ooze, marks and blemishes, then hand sanded with 320 grit.

I usually finish fumed oak with oil to deepen the colour, and sycamore with acrylic varnish to preserve its pale hue. However, as several pieces of the table could not be finished until after assembly, I decided to give it several light coats of oil, then

two coats of wax, which were buffed to a gentle sheen. The result was good, darkening the oak nicely – the slight yellowing effect on the sycamore was quite pleasing, softening the contrast a little.

Conclusion

Making this piece was interesting and proved to be good training. I felt that it worked nicely and would also work well without the contrasting timbers or the inlays. I also felt, once it was finished, that the front and back stretchers would have looked better in the higher position on the straight part of the leg – which would be much simpler to make! ■

**BELOW LEFT:
Drilling the
buttons with a
combination drill
and countersink**

**BELOW RIGHT:
Buttons in place –
an alternative
method is the
expansion plate**

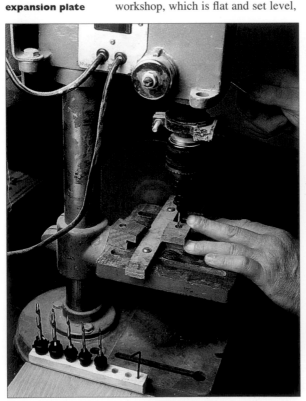

SUPPLIERS

Combined countersink and drill set – Craft Supplies Ltd, The Mill, Millers Dale, Nr Buxton, Derby SK17 8SN Tel: 01298 871636

You rang?

How to make a
butler's tray
drinks cabinet

WHILE 'RESTING' between orders some years ago I decided to make a speculative piece on the lines of a butler's table, examples of which I had seen in antique shops – they are made up of a large tray, designed for the butler to carry to and from the pantry, which fits on top of a side table. The sides of the tray are hinged so that they can be locked into an upright position when the tray is being carried. These special spring-loaded hinges are

known as 'butler's tray' hinges and are still available today.

Design
I decided to scale my butler's tray down in size and, to go underneath the tray, I designed

a small cabinet to house drinks.
So that it can be viewed from all sides, the back is solid, and the brass fittings, combined with the complex, rich figuring of the oiled burr, make a distinctive, and decorative piece.

"The brass fittings, combined with the complex, rich figuring of the oiled burr, make a distinctive, and decorative piece"

LEFT: The butler's
tray cabinet

"Timber selection is of paramount importance to the success of any piece, but never more so than with burr"

Timber selection

RIGHT: Cabinet and tray, separate

It was early on in my career that I embarked on this project, and I was aware of the risks of working in solid burr with its wild grain, faults, and readiness to move. But, mindful of the motto 'who dares, probably doesn't understand', I decided to have a go – but very carefully.

I had some burr elm (*Ulmus procera*) from a local fallen tree which I had planked and stick-dried for about two years.

Timber selection is of paramount importance to the success of any piece, but never more so than with burr. With such beautiful, but wild, figuring, it takes time and care to get the overall look right.

I checked for faults, grain direction, figuring, and colour, then cut the pieces well oversize and laid them out in their relative positions to try and get an impression of the finished effect.

To get an idea of what the colour would be like, I dressed the wood, and gave it a coat of white spirit. This produced a temporary effect similar to oil or varnish, enabling the colour to be checked and matched.

BELOW: Sides of tray showing handle and feet which act as locators

"Mindful of the motto 'who dares, probably doesn't understand', I decided to have a go – but very carefully"

Smaller pieces

Most of the pieces were cut from a single piece of burr, but I had nothing wide enough for the top, base, and back of the cabinet, or the rectangular centre section of the tray. These pieces would therefore need to be made from jointed narrower pieces.

The best way I have found for joining them is to deep-saw a thick piece and join the two resulting thinner pieces, saw faces up, as in a book-matched veneer.

The result is a balanced picture or pattern in the figuring, provided the join is centred in the width.

The wild grain left end-grain across some areas of the joins so a loose tongue of ply was used as a strengthener.

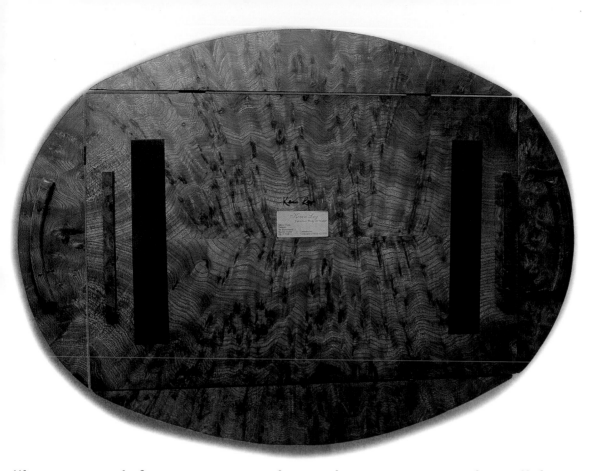

"It was not left, even overnight, without ensuring that all faces had equal free airflow around them"

Conditioning

The burr was brought into the house, sticked, and left in a warm room to condition for a month – this was in the days before my conditioning cabinet!

It was then finally dimensioned, ready for cutting out. I was careful to keep the timber in stick in my warm, dry workshop with a weight on top, throughout the whole making process. It was not left, even overnight, without ensuring that all faces had equal free airflow around them.

Cabinet carcass

The cabinet carcass is made from 16mm (⅝in) thickness timber. The top and base are cut to size, and stopped housings cut for the sides. The stopped housing cut in the base is 16mm (⅝in) wide by 10mm (⅜in) deep.

The housing in the top is 6mm (¼in) wide by 10mm (⅜in) deep and offset to allow for the tray's locating recess. The sides are shouldered to fit the housing and a rebate cut in the top of the sides to fit the offset housing in the top.

The recesses for the locating tray feet are cut in the top, on the bandsaw. The back of the cabinet is a piece of solid burr and is fitted as a floating panel into a slot cut in the top, sides, and base. All five pieces are dry fitted, finished, glued, and clamped. The back is not, of course, glued-in, so that it can move.

The carcass is checked for square, back and front, and left to set.

Doors

The door frames are made from 38mm by 22mm (1½in by ⅞in) burr, with a mortice and tenon joint at the corners. The panels are deep cut from a single thick piece, finished to ½in thickness, and book matched. To field the panel, first cut a groove 3mm (⅛in) deep, 25mm (1in) in from all the front face edges of the panel, on the circular saw, suitably lowered, to form the shoulder between the centre panel and the chamfered edge.

The majority of the waste is then removed from the edges with a router and the fielding finished with a sharp shoulder plane, leaving a raised panel in the centre. The panels, particularly the fielded edges, are finished carefully, as it is far easier to do this before they are fitted.

The frame pieces are grooved on the inside edge, to take the fielded edges of the panels, which are set

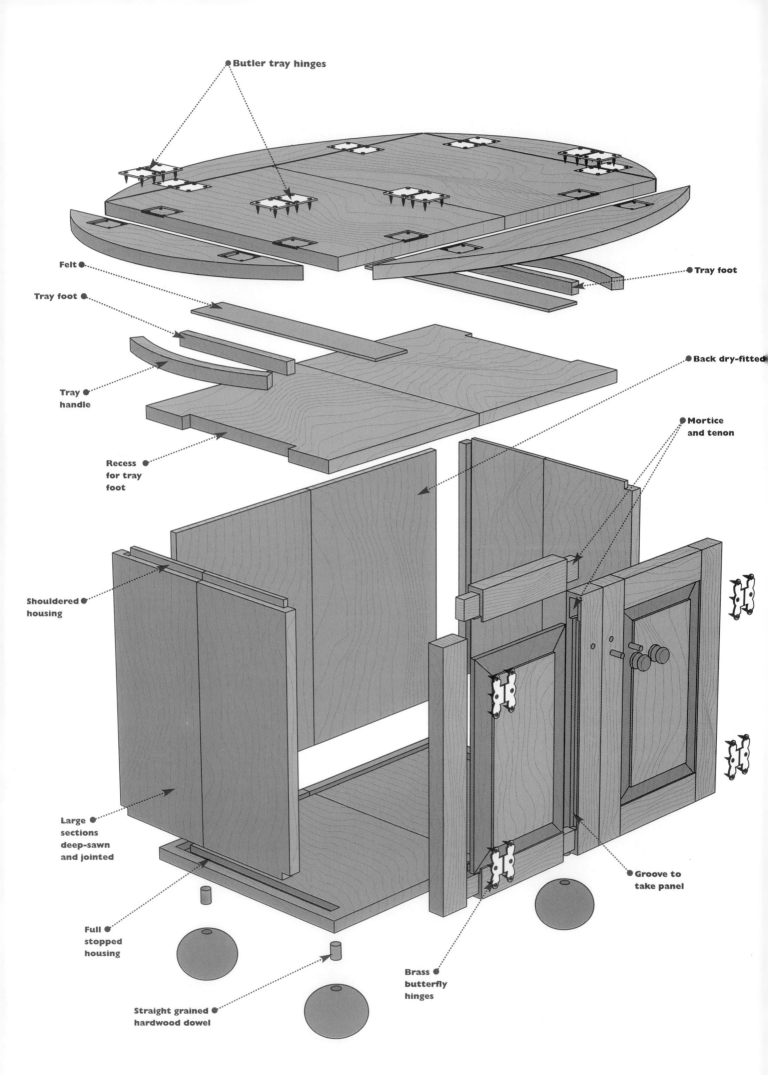

Butler tray hinges

Felt

Tray foot

Tray foot

Back dry-fitted

Tray handle

Mortice and tenon

Recess for tray foot

Shouldered housing

Large sections deep-sawn and jointed

Groove to take panel

Full stopped housing

Brass butterfly hinges

Straight grained hardwood dowel

LEFT: A fine array of single malts

"Turning the dowel as part of the pull or bun foot can be risky – the burr's wild grain may not run true along the length of the dowel, and will possibly shear in the future"

6mm (¼in) into the frame. Glue is applied to the mortices, the panels inserted dry to allow for movement, and the doors clamped and checked to see that they are square and flat, and left to cure.

Fitting
Once cured, they are fitted to the cabinet carcass using 38mm (1½in) solid brass butterfly hinges – not the cheap brassed steel versions! These give the decorative effect I wanted, and are easier to fit, not needing a recess! Leave a bit more clearance around the doors than usual to allow for the greater potential movement of the burr.

19mm (¾in) pulls are turned from an offcut of the burr and fitted. Brass double-ball catches are then put on.

While on the lathe, I turned the bun feet. The pulls and bun feet are fitted using straight-grained hardwood dowels of a suitable diameter, recessed into the pulls and the door frame, and the top of the bun foot and the base of the cabinet.

Turning the dowel as part of the pull or bun foot can be risky – the burr's wild grain may not run true along the length of the dowel, and will possibly shear in the future.

Tray construction
The tray is also constructed from 16mm (⅝in) thick timber. It is vital that it has been seasoned and conditioned well, as the tray is unbraced and has nothing to hold it if it wants to move.

The selected pieces need to be checked carefully for true. The natural shape of burrs makes it easy to choose side pieces with the grain running parallel to the curve. I tried to get the flow and colours of the figuring to run through as much as possible, as though the whole thing had been cut from one piece.

Hinges
These hinges are more difficult to fit than a normal butt hinge, so it is worth doing a trial run on two pieces of scrap to find the depths and clearances required.

The spring-loaded leaf is fitted to the centre piece of the tray, with an extra recess leaving relatively narrow shoulders to take the screws. The centre recess for the spring needs 1.5mm (¹⁄₁₆in) extra clearance for the spring to open and close during operation.

Drill the pilot holes for the brass semi-domed screws, taking particular care with the narrow shoulders. Once fitted, all the slots should line up in true military style!

The curved handles are made and spot-glued and pinned to the end pieces. Feet are cut to fit the recesses in the top and similarly fitted to the tray. These double as locators when

BELOW: Top located and sides down

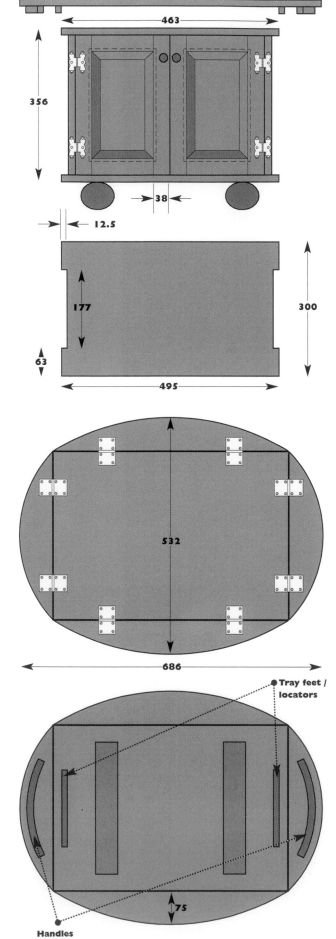

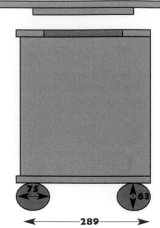

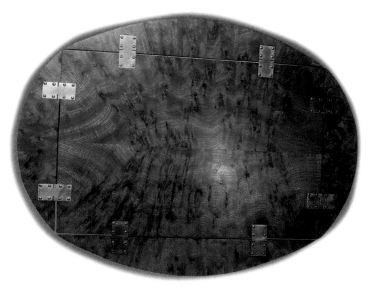

ABOVE: Brass butler's hinges look good against the rich figuring of the burr

the tray is replaced on the top. They are tapered slightly on the inside and at each end to aid an easy fit.

Finally, two broad strips of self-adhesive baize are fitted on the underside of the tray, to prevent scuff marks on the top.

Finish

An oiled finish shows off the wonderful rich colour and figure of the wood, and thoroughly seals and stabilises it as well. The satin finish hides any slight, but inevitable blemishes in the surface of the burr.

The first coat is the most important as, once it has cured, little further penetration takes place. Keep the first coat wet all day by refreshing it frequently until no more is soaked up. All surplus oil is removed with kitchen roll and the pieces left to dry for 24 hours in a warm, dry place.

A further light coat of oil is applied every 24 hours for the next week, rubbing down between coats with Scotchbrite grey pad, and allowing no build up of oil on the surface.

I found that the brass hinges tarnished with the first coat of oil and I had to remove and re-polish and re-fit them after the first coat had cured.

The advantage of the oiled finish is that it is easily renewable and improves with age and TLC – like so many of us! ■

SUPPLIERS

Butler's tray hinges and a wide range of brass fittings from:
H E Savill 9/12 St Martin's Place Scarborough North Yorkshire YO11 2Q8 tel 01723 373032 fax 01723 376984

Speculating in sy

A Shaker-influenced lady's writing desk is made from
a timber which used to be more at home in the kitchen

IN THE PAST sycamore (*Acer pseudoplatanus*) was a utilitarian wood used for draining and wash boards, butchers' blocks and kitchen tables, and other utensils which came into contact with food; the close grain and pale colour allowed surfaces to be left unsealed while bleaching and scrubbing kept everything hygienic and looking good.

The Georgians used figured sycamore as a decorative veneer on fine pieces, although generally stained grey and referred to as 'harewood'.

The first time I saw and touched natural-finished sycamore, however, I was fascinated by the silky

BELOW: Checking the slide clearance of the lady's writing desk

texture, gently understated figuring and creamy colour.

Deciding it would lend itself well to delicate work, I designed this lady's writing desk and its chair, *see 'Shaker leg'*, page 87, as a speculative piece.

Timber selection

This moderately priced British hardwood is in plentiful supply, but must be felled in winter when the sap is down, and seasoned in an upright position – 'end-reared' – after conversion to boards and before kilning.

This treatment prevents staining from the sap, and penetrating sticker marks. Ideal drying conditions are cold nights and warm sunny days.

When buying, try to obtain a guarantee that the job has been done properly because the sap staining is an ugly, dirty, grey which I have not found any satisfactory method of removing; bleaching seems to turn it an equally ugly green.

Surface staining is of a similar colour, but comes off on the first pass over the planer; so it pays to test the wood with a small plane before buying.

Good sized, clean, through-and-through boards are usually available; quarter-sawn sycamore has an interesting lacy figure which blends in well as a special feature, perhaps for drawer fronts or door panels.

Rarer and more expensive is ripple or fiddleback sycamore, much coveted for musical instruments. I feel that a little of

camore

> "The first time I saw and touched finished sycamore, however, I was fascinated by the silky texture, gently understated figuring and creamy colour"

this goes a long way in furniture; it can easily become fussy.

Design

This design is based on the traditional bonheur du jour, or small writing desk, but with a strong Shaker influence.

Space efficiency is good; with the chair placed under the table little room is taken up; the top gives a display area, the drawers good storage, and the slide under the top a decent extra writing surface.

The desk slips easily into most settings in most houses, being particularly useful in small rooms or niches, so making an excellent hall or telephone table.

The pieces pictured here have been displayed at local exhibitions, and design developments have evolved from both.

Table construction

Mortise the legs before tapering, and begin the taper 150mm, 6in down from the top of the leg. The tapers can be achieved with jigs on the planer-thicknesser or circular saw; but I find the simplest, safest, and most enjoyable method is to rough them out on the bandsaw and finish by hand, as the wood is such a joy to plane.

Round over the feet of the legs, *see fig 1*. Cut the tenons on the front drawer rail, sides, and back.

Before assembly recess the sides and front legs to take the slide. The sides and back should have recesses cut for the expansion brackets to which the top will attach; make sure that those in the sides are set well back to clear the slide.

The position of the brackets should be set just below the level of the top, so that it is pulled

tightly down onto the sides and back when fixed.

Fit the brackets' faces with countersunk holes into these recesses; make them a snug fit as movement need not be allowed for at this point.

Suspension runners

The drawer suspension runners should also be made and fitted

now. To ensure accurate running of the drawers, cut a test slot in a piece of scrap using the router cutter that will later be used to slot the drawer sides. Dimension the runners to fit tightly into this, so that only micro adjustment will be necessary later.

Screw and glue them into place on the sides.

Dry fit all the joints before

BELOW: A light and simple design, with interest added by the contrasting fumed oak pulls and the writing slide

"Make sure the screws don't inadvertently go right through the top!"

gluing, finishing all the surfaces as far as possible. Glue and clamp the sides to the legs, checking for square, and leave to set. When dry these two sub-assemblies are joined by gluing and clamping the back and the front drawer rail to the legs; again check for square in all directions and leave to set.

Prepare top

Prepare the top for fitting by cutting recesses for the expansion brackets. The bracket's slotted faces are fitted to the top; make sure the screws are placed in the correct slots to allow movement across the grain!

The recesses must be oversize in the direction of movement – front to back and vice versa – to allow for expansion or contraction of the top. Be very careful to ensure that the brackets are set deep enough to allow the slide to move without fouling the brackets or the screw heads.

Cut two slots in the underside of the top to take the slide stop screws, *see next paragraph*; they should stop 75mm (3in) back from the front of the top. Fit the top to the brackets, making sure the screws don't inadvertently go right through the top!

Drawer and slide

The drawer also fulfils the function of lopers in that it supports the slide when extended. To achieve this, fit two fixed dowels to the underside of the slide, projecting downwards and

set back 75mm (3in) from the front. These engage the drawer front as the slide is pulled out, causing the drawer to be opened with it, thus providing the necessary support, *see fig 2*.

The drawer is of traditional construction The drawer casings are cedar (*Cedrus libani*), and the bottom 4mm, $^5/_{32}$in cedar-

veneered MDF. The sides are slotted to take the runners using the router cutter mentioned above.

The drawer should be fitted carefully; as it takes the weight of the slide, play between the runners and slot should be as small as possible while allowing free movement. Finally cut two

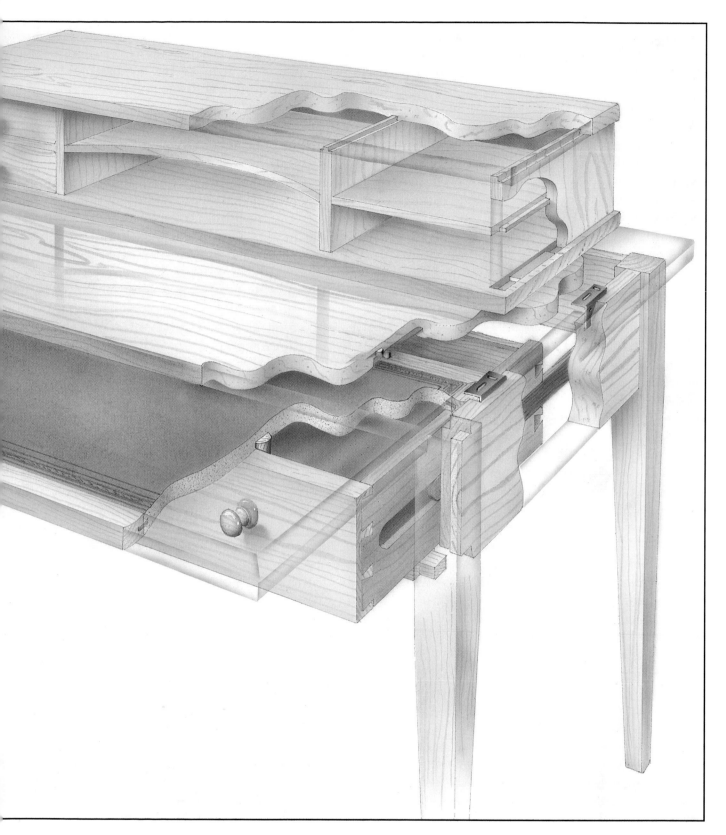

scallops out of the back of the drawer to allow it to be fitted and removed without fouling the slide's dowels.

To prevent the slide being pulled right out, fit two filed-down screws through its back edge; these run in the stopped slots cut earlier in the underside of the top, *see above*.

These are screwed into place after the slide has been positioned and before the drawer is fitted.

Check the slide carefully for clearance; to prevent any scuffing of its skiver when it is in use, the underside of the table top should be covered with a piece of baize.

Top carcass

The top carcass is a straight-forward construction in 10mm, (3/8in) thick stock with backs of 4mm (5/32in) sycamore-veneered MDF. The drawer unit can be fixed to the top in a number of ways; that shown is by shouldered tenons through the base, let in to mortises in the table top.

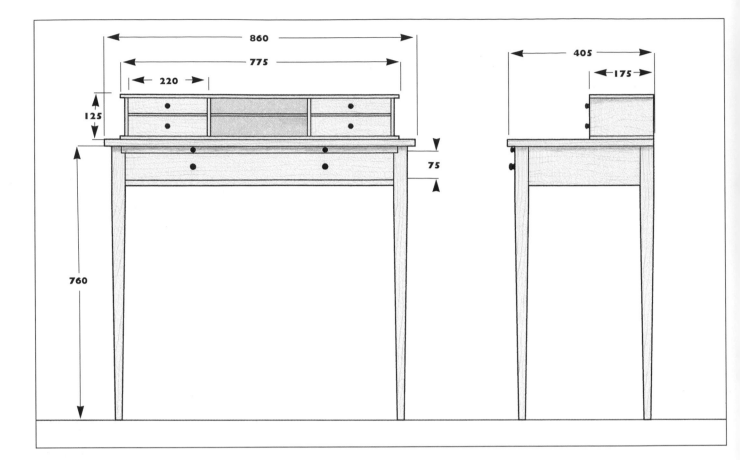

Brackets, dowels or screws could be used on the back edges. One client wanted the option of removing the drawer unit, and did not want the top defaced, so we located it on the top with Blu-Tack to stop it slipping, a technique which I understand is still satisfactory!

Dimension all the pieces and cut mortises in the top and bottom to take the uprights – remembering to make the appropriate through cuts in the base for the shouldered tenons, if required.

Mortise the uprights to take the shelves, and slot them for the backs. Tenon the uprights and shelves, and cut the curved front on the middle shelf.

Dry assemble all the joints to check the fit, and finish all the pieces. Gluing up is a little tricky, and I used the following method, *see photo:* glue the shelves and backs in to the uprights – do not glue the tops or bottoms of the backs – and dry fit the top and bottom; pull up the shelf and back joints with sash cramps back and front; check for square and leave to set.

When dry, carefully remove the top and bottom, apply glue to the joints and re-fit them. Clamp them up, check for square and leave to set.

Make and fit the drawers – again the casings are cedar and the bottoms cedar-veneered MDF, glued in all round.

Contrasting detail

To provide extra detail interest to the piece I use a contrasting timber such as rosewood (*Dalbergia sp*), or in this case fumed oak (*Quercus robur*), for the knobs. Turn and finish the pieces on the lathe, using a sizing tool to make the spigots, oil and fit.

Finishing

Check all the joints for glue squeeze-out, then clean up ready for the finish. I apply three coats of an acrylic water-based varnish – preferably one with a UV filter incorporated to minimise yellowing or darkening – to the sycamore; rub down to denib between coats.

Fit the knobs and the leather skiver; and finish with two coats of clear wax, buffing to a gentle sheen.

Conclusion

The small mechanical element made this an interesting piece to build, and one that has enjoyed success in several directions. I still have the prototype in my house – and it continues to generate work.

Shaker leg

The perfect companion to a lady's writing desk, this Shaker-influenced chair was made to complete the set

"Harewood was derived from 'air-wood', being as light as air"

THIS IS VERY much a Shaker design, the tapers on the legs and rails and the thin seat-frame keeping it light and dainty. Sycamore is especially appropriate; its Georgian name 'harewood' was derived from 'air-wood', being as light as air.

The light construction does, however, require great accuracy and care in the jointing to ensure that it can withstand the severe stresses placed on a chair – even one to be used by a lady!

Plans

First make a set of full-size drawings – plan and elevations – on a piece of hardboard or similar, from which the angles of the joints and precise dimensions may be taken.

Cut the legs to size, cut all the mortises, and drill the 13mm

ABOVE RIGHT: The chair with its companion writing table

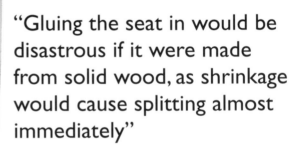

"Gluing the seat in would be disastrous if it were made from solid wood, as shrinkage would cause splitting almost immediately"

(½in) holes for the stretchers. The top of the back legs can be drilled for the finials at this stage.

Taper the front legs, and 150mm (6in) each end of the back legs. I hand plane these after roughing out on the bandsaw as sycamore is so workable, but a tapering jig can be made for most static machines if preferred. Slot the inside corners of the legs to accept the seat, *see illustration*; then radius the tops and bottoms – except the top inside edges of the mortised faces – of the front legs.

Make the seat frame-rails, cutting the tenons at the angle required for the front to back taper of the seat. This angle can be measured from the full-size

LEFT: Fumed oak finials are spigoted into holes in the back legs

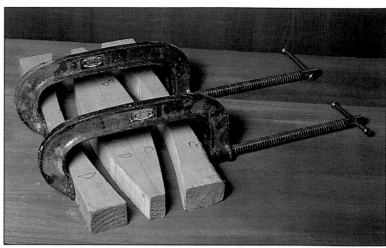

ABOVE: A simple former for producing the steam-bent back rails

"The fumed oak finials are turned with spigots to fit the holes in the top of the back legs"

plan drawing. Cut the stretchers to length from 19mm by 19mm (³/₄in by ³/₄in) stock. The taper on these runs from 19mm (³/₄in) at the centre to 13mm (¹/₂in) at the ends; I use a sizing tool on the lathe to ensure the ends are a consistent good fit. If no lathe is available these components can be shaped using a spoke shave, but pay careful attention to the diameter of the ends where they are jointed into the legs.

Curved rails
From 8mm, ⁵/₁₆in stock cut four back rails – one spare just in case! – work the tenons' shoulders and cut the top curve while these parts are flat. Steam for about 30 minutes before clamping to a former, *see photo*, giving about 19mm (³/₄in) of

curavture at the centre.

Leave overnight to set; then angle and finish the tenons with a small hand plane to fit the 6mm (¹/₄in) mortises in the back legs.

Dry fit all the joints, make any necessary adjustments and then finish all the individual components; glue, assemble and clamp the back and front sub-assemblies. Check for square and leave to set.

Cut the seat to size from 6mm (¹/₄in) sycamore-veneered ply or MDF; cut out the leg rebates in its corners.

Assembly
Finish assembling the chair by gluing and clamping the side seat rails and stretchers to the back and front; with the seat glued into its slot all round. Once

again check for square and leave to set.

Gluing the seat in would be disastrous if it were made from solid wood, as shrinkage would cause splitting almost immediately. As ours is made of stable veneered material, though, it will strengthen the structure and remove the need for corner braces.

The fumed oak finials are turned with spigots to fit the holes in the top of the back legs, and are glued in place.

The seat can be used as it is or with a loose or tie-on cushion.

■ See previous project, 'Speculating in sycamore', for details of the accompanying writing desk

Window dressing

How to make an elm and burr-elm coffer chest

I APPROACHED A newly opened local department store and suggested that the creation of a 'craftsman' window display would help it to identify with the local community. The display, I thought, should consist of some rich, unusual pieces of furniture, shown alongside wooden tools and shavings, and would result in welcome publicity for us both; I would pay them a percentage of any sales. The company liked the idea and gave me a window for three weeks.

One of the pieces I put in it was this coffer chest made in a mixture of local elm (*Ulmus procera*) and burr elm. I sold two of them in a week.

"The display was a great success and I sold two of them in a week"

Design

I had some elm with a good burr on the outside edge, becoming plain wild-grained elm towards the heart. This yielded some nice small pieces of burr along with quite a lot of matching elm.

I developed this variation on the basic chest using the small pieces of burr for the floating panels and the plainer elm for the framing.

Removable cedar of Lebanon (*Cedrus libani*) trays were included to make better use of the storage space, add interest, and give off the timber's wonderful and moth-repelling scent.

Timber selection

I like to use burr timber that would otherwise be burnt. It also seems to have both a conversational and conservational appeal to customers – particularly locals. This butt had been brought to me by my firewood supplier, Martin. It was then planked at a local sawmill and stick-dried in my timber store.

The final look of any piece is decided with the initial timber selection, never more so than when using burr. Look for grain flow, figure, faults, colour changes, dead knots and so on – I cut oversize pieces, marking each with its provisional position, and put them into the conditioning cabinet/kiln for a month or so.

I prepared enough for three chests just in case, and because one was required by Senior Management for display and use in our house.

"Because finishing can produce a marked change from the dry colour, treatment with white spirit to get a temporary idea of the likely final colour can be worthwhile"

LEFT: Sold from the window – note the full-width piano hinge for the lid, which has a smaller overhang at the back to act as a stop

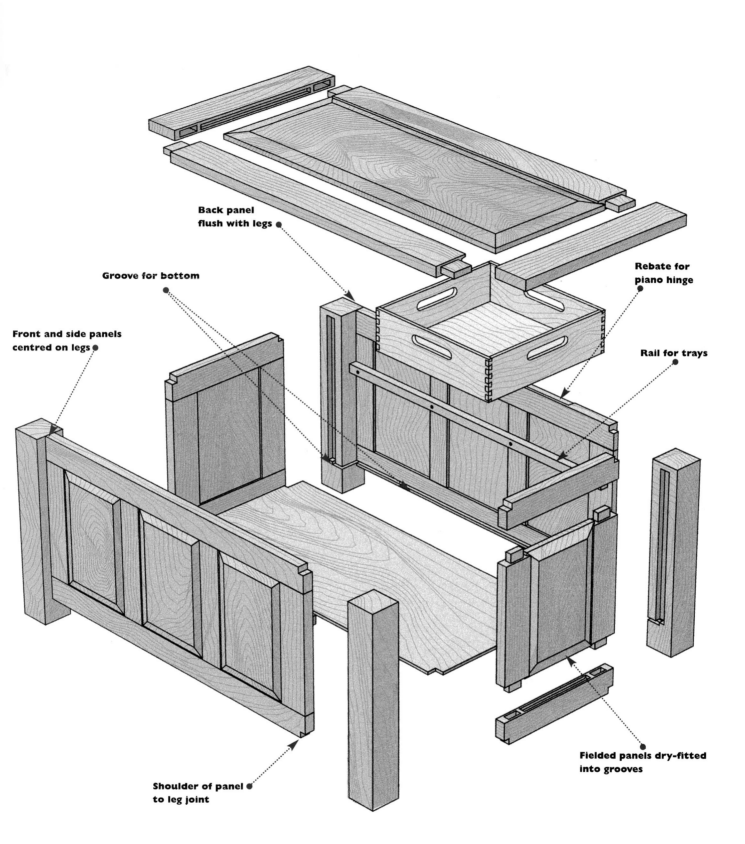

Back panel flush with legs ●

Groove for bottom ●

Front and side panels centred on legs ●

Rebate for piano hinge ●

Rail for trays ●

Shoulder of panel to leg joint ●

Fielded panels dry-fitted into grooves ●

Cutting out

I laid out the oversize, conditioned pieces, moved them around until I was happy, then marked them, but still oversize, ready for machining and final dimensioning.

Once machined it could be finally selected, using white spirit to simulate the wood's polished colour,

then stacked in stick in the warm, dry workshop so that it continued to dry evenly during the making.

The tops of the stacks were weighted to hold the timber flat as it settled. This is particularly important with elm – not known for its stability! Final dimensioning was done just before use.

Framing

The basic carcass construction is of frames with floating panels, let into corner-post legs. The frames are made from 22mm (⅞in) stock; the stiles are let in to the legs by 13mm (½in) and are cut 63mm (2½in) wide; the rails and muntins are 50mm (2in) wide. This gives a

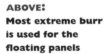

visible 50mm (2in) frame once
assembled.

The rails are morticed, and the
stiles tenoned to fit. The fielded
panels are dimensioned to allow a
6mm (¼in) tongue all round to be let
in to the frames.

The fielding is achieved by first
cutting a groove 3mm (⅛in) deep,
25mm (1in) in from all the front face

"Burr elm that would otherwise end up
as logs seems to have both a
conversational and conservational
appeal to customers"

edges of the panel using the
sawbench; this forms the shoulder
between fielding and centre panel.

The majority of the waste is then
removed from the areas to be
fielded with a router and the
low chamfer finished with a
very sharp shoulder plane. The
panels, particularly the fielded
edges, are best sealed and
polished at this point as it is
far easier to do it before they
are fitted.

The frame members are then
slotted with a 6mm (¼in) deep
groove to take the panels,
everything checked and fitted
dry, and finished.

The frames, with the panels
in place, are then glued up,
assembled, checked for square
and left to set. I put a small
blob of glue at the centre of
the top and bottom of each
panel, inside the housing, to
hold them centrally and make
sure that any movement is
equalised on each side.

Carcass

The legs are cut to length from
63mm square (2½in square) section.

A 13mm (½in) shoulder is cut on
the top and bottom of each frame,
see diagram, and a 22mm (⅞in)
housing, 13mm (½in) deep, cut in the
centre of each leg to take the front
and side framed panels.

To allow the lid to hinge, the back
panel must be fitted flush to the
backs of the legs. A 10mm (⅜in)
thick, 13mm (½in) deep tenon is
formed by rebating the outside edge
of the back frame stiles, and a
matching mortice, set back 12mm
(½in) from the back edge, is cut in
the relevant faces of the back legs,
see diagram.

I decided to hinge the top with
piano hinge for strength. This is
rebated fully into the carcass, then
fitted straight on to the underside of
the top. Having cut this rebate in the
top of the back panel, the front, sides
and back can be dry-fitted to the legs
and adjusted if necessary.

A groove is now cut in the sides,

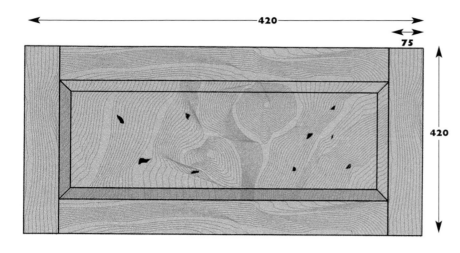

420

75

420

Lid

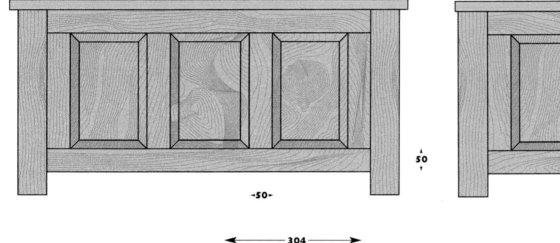

22

406

50

-50-

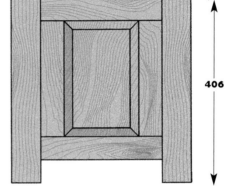

304

Carcass plan view

395

22

63

840

back, front and legs to take the bottom, which is made from 6mm (¼in) cedar of Lebanon-faced MDF. The bottom is cut to size, allowing for the groove, and cut-outs made for the legs.

The base is checked, fitted dry and adjustments made. The front and back frames and the legs are finished, glued up, fitted, clamped, checked for square and left to set. The sides and base can then also be glued up, fitted

to the legs, checked for square, and the whole carcass left to set.

Incidentally, as the MDF base is not subject to movement, it can be glued in all round for strength.

Lid

To make a panel big enough for the framed-up lid, two sequential boards of elm are book-matched and joined. If this is not possible, then the lid could have a number of panels

"At this point I checked that the lid closed down evenly all around on to the top of the carcass"

like the back and front. I felt this would give too repetitive a look – but needs must when the devil drives!

TOP RIGHT:
Cedar trays have
handles on all
four sides. The
veneered MDF
bottoms are
glued in

The top frame is 75mm (3in) wide, also of 22mm (⅞in) stock, the stiles morticed, and the rails tenoned into them; the floating fielded panel is fitted into a 10mm (⅜in) deep groove. Assembly is as for the carcass panels.

The lid overlaps the sides and front of the legs by 19mm (¾in), and the back by 6mm (¼in); this arrangement holds the lid open just past the vertical.

The lid may then be fitted to the carcass's piano hinge, which is set flush in the rebate already cut in the back top edge. At this point I check that the lid closes evenly down to the top of the carcass, and make any necessary adjustments.

Trays

The trays are made from 8mm (⁵⁄₁₆in) thick cedar of Lebanon and are of similar construction to a drawer, but with through dovetails back and front. The sides, back, and front are cut to size, through dovetailed, and grooved for the 4mm cedar of Lebanon-faced MDF bottom.

The handle cut-outs are made in all four sides of each tray with a router. Cutting from both faces will avoid break-out in this brittle timber.

The trays are then glued up and assembled with the base glued in all round for strength, checked for square and left to set.

Rails of 19mm by 19mm (¾in by ¾in) elm, on which the trays will sit, are screwed 113mm (4½in) down from the top of the carcass, giving 25mm (1in) clearance above. Once they are set the outsides of the trays can be finished.

They are then fitted in the carcass and checked to ensure even sitting on the rails.

Pleasing result

Difficulty of making does not necessarily enhance a design. This is a fairly simple piece, a bit repetitive in the making perhaps, but nevertheless giving a pleasing result.

The elm and burr pieces should even be relatively easy to harvest from potential firewood supplies, the only requirements being much patience while it dries out and seasons, care in the conditioning and selection, and enjoyment in the making.

Add to that the nice warm feeling of getting something beautiful for nothing – and what more could one ask for? ■

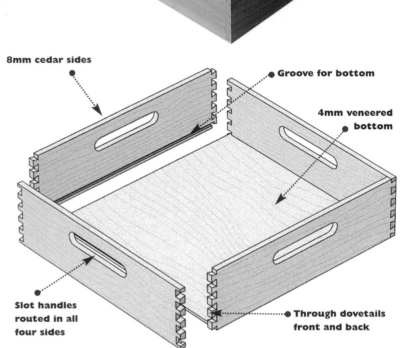

8mm cedar sides

Groove for bottom

4mm veneered bottom

Slot handles routed in all four sides

Through dovetails front and back

FINISH

I decided on a wax finish over Danish oil to see how it would look. The burr and the elm can be quite porous and oil penetrates well in to the wood, helping to stabilise it by slowing down moisture take-up and loss. Wax gives a pleasant sheen and smell and its future care is generally understood.

The first coat of oil is liberally applied, left to soak in and refreshed every 15 to 20 minutes until it will take no more – four to six coats.

It is then wiped off with a soft cloth to prevent any oil build up on the surface, and left to harden for 24 hours in a warm dry place.

The surface is cut back with a Scotchbrite grey pad and three further light coats of oil applied at 24-hour intervals. The last coat is then cut back, two coats of wax applied and buffed off with a soft cloth.

Future care is the usual light waxing. I was very pleased with the result and will use this finish again on elm.

The inside surfaces, particularly of the burr, are also oiled in a similar way, but not waxed. The outsides of the trays are lightly waxed, the insides being left untreated to let the smell out!

Curved and fumed

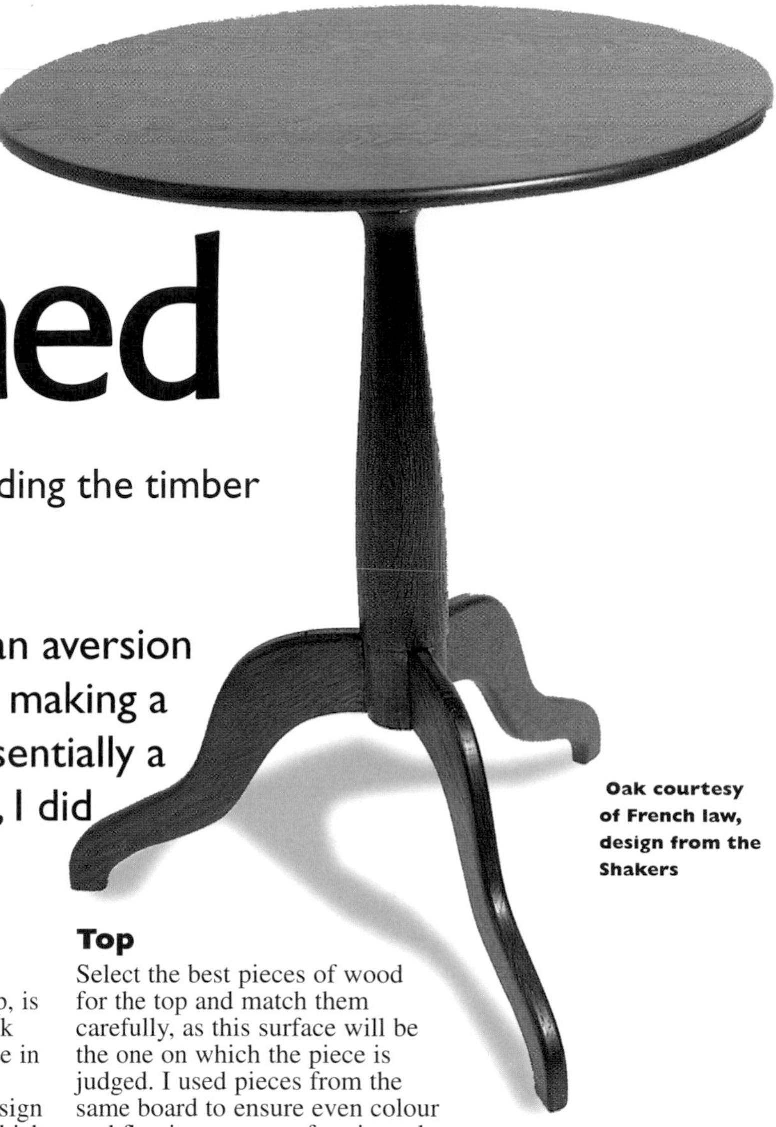

French foresight is given thanks for providing the timber for this fumed oak table

ILLUSTRATIONS BY SIMON RODWAY

IN THE DISTANT past the French were required by law to plant two oaks for every one they cut down, so ensuring plentiful future supplies for warships. This exercise in forward planning resulted in many of the trees being planted close together in stands, a method which encourages tall straight growth with a clean bole.

With warships now built from steel, furniture-makers can take advantage of this good husbandry to reap the benefits, in this case some very nice quarter-sawn French oak (*Quercus robur*).

The wood is mild, clean and straight-grained, with a good figure and consistent colour. The minimum available board thickness is generally 28mm (1^1/$_8$in), giving scope for thicker finished pieces. I took advantage of this for the top of the table.

> "Because I have an aversion to spending time making a jig for what is essentially a small one-off job, I did it by hand"

Design

My client, who specified the height and diameter of the top, is particularly fond of fumed oak and wanted a Shaker influence in the piece.

The starting point for the design was a Shaker round stand on which candles would have been placed; this would more usually have had double arc tapered legs, but we decided on the double-curved or serpentine legs shown here.

The column profile takes on a soft curve in keeping with the leg shape.

The top has a substantial 22mm (^{7}/$_8$in) section to provide strength, the edge being bevelled down to 16mm (^{5}/$_8$in) to maintain the delicate look.

The edges of the top and legs are rounded over to improve the highlights of the oiled finish and generally enhance the look and feel of the piece.

LEFT: Match the grain of the top carefully – only quarter-sawn oak should be used for this unsupported table top

Oak courtesy of French law, design from the Shakers

Top

Select the best pieces of wood for the top and match them carefully, as this surface will be the one on which the piece is judged. I used pieces from the same board to ensure even colour and flowing pattern of grain and figure, these factors being especially important when fuming.

Check that the pieces are truly quarter-sawn, with the grain running vertically through the thickness of the board, to ensure stability and minimum future movement.

After matching, plane the edges slightly hollow at the centre so that the ends pull up tight when clamped. Check that the top is flat with a straight edge, and leave to set.

Cut the brace to size, curving the ends to follow the top edge. Drill a 25mm (1in) hole in the centre to take the turned end of the column.

Cutting bevels

The bevels on the underside of the top and the brace can either be cut on the lathe – if a big enough example is available – or by using jigs on standing machines or even the router.

My lathe is not large enough and, because I have an aversion

TOP: Underside of table showing brace connecting the column to the top

"I drew the leg freehand in chalk until I was happy with the shape and curves, pencilled it in, then cut it out as a pattern"

FAR RIGHT: Ease the legs into their housings with glue as a lubricant

RIGHT: Routing the dovetail housings while the column is mounted on the lathe, using a simple jig

to spending time making a jig for what is essentially a small one-off job, I did this by hand. Mark the width and depth of the bevel, sharpen up the smoothing plane, clamp the work to the bench and, with a coarseish but comfortable set to the plane, remove the bulk of the waste. When close to the lines, re-sharpen and set the plane, finishing to the line – much more satisfying than all that noise and dust!

To finish off, round over the top edge of the top to 6mm ($^{1}/_{4}$in) radius with the router and soften the bottom edge with a sanding block.

Brace preparation

Position the brace on the underside of the top with the grain running at right angles. Prepare four slots – or oversized holes with spacing washers to allow for movement – for the screws.

As this wood was kiln-dried quarter-sawn, and the diameter of the top is quite small, the amount of movement is also likely to be minimal.

In this case I used a hole countersunk from each side; this provides a neat result with enough purchase to hold the top down, and allows some side-to-side movement.

Put the brace aside for later fitting to the column.

Column

Cut the column blank to size and turn it to shape – a gentle tapering curve from top to bottom looks less severe than a straight taper and is more compatible with the double curved legs.

LEVELLING THE LEGS

WHILE A three-legged table will always have all its legs on the ground and won't rock, it is more difficult to level. The best way is to stand it on a known level surface – I keep a 6ft by 4ft piece of 1in MDF, levelled as a reference surface, on the workshop floor – and check with a spirit level.

Wedge up one or two feet as necessary to achieve the level, and adjust until only one foot is wedged to retain the level, reducing the other two feet by that amount.

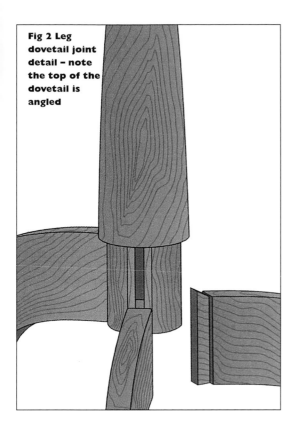

Fig 2 Leg
dovetail joint
detail – note
the top of the
dovetail is
angled

"This joint is a bit fiddly to achieve, but a little cautious practice on pieces of scrap helps avoid disaster so make haste slowly!"

The fixing peg on the top is best finished with a sizing tool to ensure a good all-round fit. Using the sizing tool on the leg recess as well achieves a good straight line for the leg joints.

Leg joints

The running dovetail housing for the legs is most easily cut while the column is still on the lathe. For this I think it is worthwhile making a simple jig – I have had full value out of mine!

The precise arrangement depends on lathe and router, but the principle is a fixed stand attached to the lathe, supporting a sliding table to which the router is attached. This enables a housing groove to be cut in the leg recess.

Use of a reference point or indexing on the lathe enables work to be turned through 120° twice to make the three housings.

To achieve a dovetail housing first remove most of the waste with a smaller straight cutter before a final pass with a 13mm

($^{1}/_{2}$in) dovetail cutter. This avoids overloading the router, and/or breaking the dovetail cutter – the whole dovetail shape must be cut in one pass; the undercut does not allow a number of shallow passes to be made.

The resulting housings, 13mm ($^{1}/_{2}$in) wide at the bottom of the cut by 13mm ($^{1}/_{2}$in) deep, could be cut by hand with a fine tenon saw and finished with a chisel, but they would take very careful marking out, great care, a long time and are unlikely to be as accurate as those cut with the router.

Legs

Cut a piece of hardboard 270mm (10$^{1}/_{2}$in) wide by 260mm (10in) high and mark the outline of the leg on it through the diagonal – this results in the tenon end for the running dovetail being at right angles to the base of the foot; be sure to allow for the dovetail tenon on the width.

RIGHT: Fig I
Only six
components
make this
table

I drew the leg freehand in chalk until I was happy with the shape and curves, pencilled it in, then cut it out as a pattern.

Cut out three legs from 19mm ($^{3}/_{4}$in) stock, ensuring the grain direction runs at 45° top to bottom. This gives maximum strength by avoiding short grain anywhere. Round over the edges

"Do not let any oil build up on the surface as it will quickly look syrupy and spoil the effect – less is best"

ABOVE: The desired effect

of the legs to a 6mm ($^1/4$in) radius, and finish.

Dovetail tenon

To fit the legs to the column either the shoulders of the leg tenons must be undercut to allow for the curve of the column or the column's face must be flattened with a sharp chisel. I find the latter much easier.

A $^3/4$in chisel centred over the housing should give the exact width of face required. This joint is a bit fiddly to achieve, but a little cautious practice on pieces of scrap helps avoid disaster, so make haste slowly!

With the dovetail cutter that was used for the housing, and the router mounted on its table, set the fence so that each side of the leg tenon end can be run against it to cut each side of the tenon.

This is not as difficult to set up as might be thought – perform test runs to check fit by using some scraps of the stock from which the legs were cut. In the absence of a router table, the router can, with extreme care, be used hand-held with its side

fence on the leg, this being held in a vice.

The top of the dovetail should be angled to match the sides; fitting the housing end left by the rotary dovetail cutter, *see illustration.*

Assembly

Apply glue to the inside of the dovetail housing and, using the glue as a lubricant, slide the legs into position. Make sure they are pushed tightly home, and leave to set.

Glue and fit the central hole in the brace over the peg on the column; pull down and strengthen the joint by countersinking two $1^1/2$in No. 8 screws through the brace, down into the column, either side of and parallel to the peg. Leave to set.

Lastly, with the top face down on a soft, padded surface, screw the brace to the top through the prepared holes.

Finishing

All pieces should be finished and sanded as far as possible before assembly. Before fuming, all

surplus glue must be cleaned off, particularly from around the joints. Check the whole piece carefully for marks, blemishes, rough spots, raised grain etc.

Prepare a polythene tent to fit over the table, ensuring that it is clear of all surfaces of the table, and place about 5fl oz of 880 ammonia in a container inside. If in a reasonably warm place, leave overnight, if cold, leave for 48 hours.

Oiling really suits oak. Apply a liberal coat, refreshing it as necessary until it will take no more; wipe off all surplus, buff and leave to dry in a warm, dry place for 24 hours.

Give a further light coat every 24 hours until the desired effect is achieved; four or five coats are usually enough. Do not let any oil build up on the surface as it will quickly look syrupy and spoil the effect – less is best.

Conclusion

Though a relatively simple piece with only six components and six joints, it is interesting, demanding and rewarding to make.

The fumed and oiled oak is resilient and ages well. The inevitable marks and bruises that will occur can be 'oiled in' to give real character with time and tender loving care!

Present and correct

How to make a military-style chest

ILLUSTRATIONS BY SIMON RODWAY

Originally conceived as travelling chests for the military, they can make attractive storage pieces

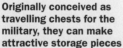

Side, showing recessed brass handles

I made an English military-style chest in oak (*Quercus robur*) several years ago for a client and when he rang to ask for another one, to be an exact copy of the first, I was pretty confident it could be done. I went to find the drawings, one of the first set I had done on the computer and, needless to say, they were nowhere to be found. Fortunately, I have kept a photographic record of everything that I have made since I started. I found the prints and worked out the measurements from what I remembered, and what I could deduce, by scaling and measuring the photos. I produced a drawing and sent it to the client for confirmation of the measurements – and it was spot on!

Carcass construction

The top is made up first from three of the best widths – the figure is matched carefully to run through and disguise the join, and the joint is strengthened with

"I found the prints and worked out the measurements from what I remembered, and what I could deduce, by scaling and measuring the photos"

Timber

The client lives in a converted barn where the internal oak frame has been sand-blasted to expose the wood. He was particularly keen on the chest being of English oak, including some of the paler sapwood, to match that in the house.

A trip to my usual timber merchant and a root through their stocks of English oak, and I found just what was needed. The timber was delivered to my workshop, sticked, stacked, and left to condition for a couple of weeks. It was then faced and thicknessed to 22mm (⅞in), all the pieces selected, marked in chalk, and cut out slightly over-size. Through the whole making process any wood not actually being worked on was stacked on stickers in the workshop to avoid any uneven drying and subsequent distortion.

Interior view

biscuits. The edges are planed on the surfacer, finished by hand to remove the ripples, and left slightly hollow in the middle, so that when clamped, the ends will be under pressure. This allows for extra shrinkage at the ends as the end-grain loses water more quickly.

When set, it is cut to exact size and a 10mm (⅜in) deep by 5mm (¼in) wide slot cut to take the top of the oak-faced MDF back, allowing for an overhang of 25mm (1in) to the back and each side.

Next, stopped housings are cut to take the sides, again allowing for the 25mm (1in) overhang.

Sides and base

The sides and base are made up in the same way as the top from carefully matched pieces. They are cut to size and

the slot is cut in the sides for the MDF back. The top drawer frame stopped housing, 10mm (⅜) wide by 10mm (⅜in) deep, is offset down to leave room for the side tenon into the top, then the 22mm (⅞in) wide by 10mm (⅜in) deep stopped housings for the remaining two drawer frames and the base are cut.

The housings to take the feet are cut in the front, set back 6mm (¼in) and up to the stopped housing for the base. The tops of the sides are shouldered to fit into the stopped housings in the top. The shape of the feet are cut in the bottom edges of the sides on the bandsaw and finished with plane, chisel, and scraper.

The base is shouldered to fit the stopped housing in the sides and the housings for the feet are cut in the underside.

Drawer frames

The drawer frames are made up from 64 by 22mm (2½ by ⅞in) oak, with biscuited joints and shouldered front and back, to go into the stopped housings in the sides. The front biscuits are glued but those at the back are not, and an expansion gap is left to allow for movement in the sides. The unglued biscuits in the back were a bit loose so I gave them a short soaking in water to swell them sufficiently to make a tight fit, tapped into position with a mallet. The top frame sides are rebated to 10mm (⅜in) for the offset top housing.

Assembly

The carcass is assembled with the drawer frames glued into the housings in the front and back of the carcass sides,

Drawers

All the pieces for the drawers are cut to size, fitted and marked. The fronts are from 22mm (⅞in) oak, the carcasses from 10mm (⅜in) oak, and the bases from 5mm (⅛in) oak-faced MDF. The sides are slotted for the bases, taped together in pairs, with the top one marked out in pencil, and the tails cut on the bandsaw.

The pins are marked on the drawer fronts and backs, one at a time, from the corresponding tails, and the majority of the waste removed with a router. Each joint is then individually finished with a sharp chisel. It is easier to fit the recessed brass handles into the fronts, before assembling the drawers, so a hardboard template is made. The positions are marked out, the correct depth set on the router, and the recesses cut out freehand. The handles are check-fitted and removed, to be permanently fixed after finishing.

Each drawer is then assembled, with the MDF base glued in all round and pinned at the back, checked for square and wind, and left to set. The drawers are then finally fitted, finished and put on one side.

Foot detail

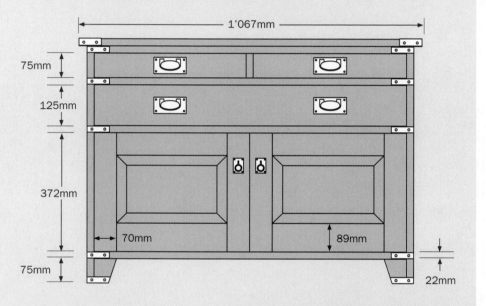

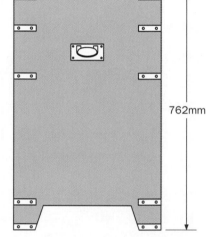

leaving the sides of the frames a dry, running fit in the sides of the carcass, to allow for future movement. The base is glued all along the stopped housing, as the grain run is in the same direction as the sides.

The back and top are dry-fitted to help keep everything square. Clamps are applied, the diagonals measured front and back to check it is square, adjustments made, and left to set.

Once dry, the upright between the two top drawers is fitted by screwing through the frames above and below. The screws are deep countersunk, and plugs of oak fitted to hide them. The feet are cut to size and shape, and glued into position in the slots in the sides and base.

I prefer to fit tops upside down where possible to stop any glue running out of

the housings. The top is placed on padded trestles with the stopped housings uppermost, glue is applied, and the carcass lowered so that the tops of the sides fit into the housings. Clamp it, check for square and leave to set.

The oak-faced MDF back is then glued into the slots in the sides and top, and glued and pinned to the backs of the drawer rails and the base.

Doors

Check the measurements of the front opening of the cupboard and cut the stiles and rails of the doors to size. I had previously checked a double biscuit joint to destruction and was satisfied with its strength, so decided to use it here.

The doors are dry-assembled and the measurements for the fielded panels

"I prefer to fit tops upside down where possible to stop any glue running out of the housings"

taken, allowing them to recess 6mm (¼in) into the frame.

The door panels are made up by deep-sawing some selected figured oak and match jointing with biscuits, for extra strength, in the middle. This produces a pleasing effect in the figure and the colour.

The panels are cut to size and fielded using a vertical profile cutter, keeping

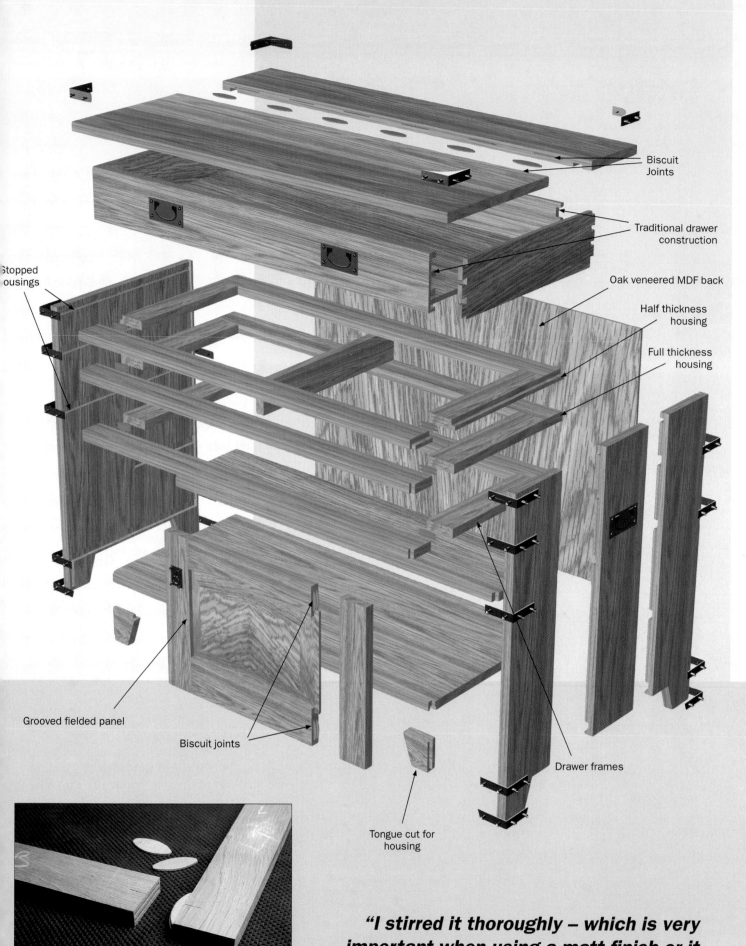

Biscuit
Joints

Traditional drawer
construction

Oak veneered MDF back

Half thickness
housing

Full thickness
housing

Stopped
housings

Drawer frames

Grooved fielded panel

Biscuit joints

Tongue cut for
housing

Double biscuit joints have proved to be more than
adequate as an alternative to loose tenons

*"I stirred it thoroughly – which is very
important when using a matt finish or it
will 'gloss up' – unevenly!"*

Fitting doors

Once set, the faces of the frames are finished, and the completed doors fitted to opening, leaving about 1mm (1/16in) clearance all round, to be adjusted to 2mm (1/8in) on fitting.

The hinges are recessed into the door only, and not the carcass side, leaving a neater line. They are positioned on the frame and scribed round with a scalpel. The router fence and depth are set to take out the majority of the waste, and the recesses squared off, using the scalpel line as a register for the chisel.

The brass butt hinges are cleaned and polished on the visible faces to take out the machine marks, and screwed into the recess. I used a self-centring hinge pilot drill, and my power screw driver, both of which I swear by.

The position of the hinges is marked on the inside face of the cupboard, and a cutting gauge used to scribe the screw line. The doors are held at the correct height by a metal rule wedged as a spacer underneath them.

The screw line is centred in the hinge screw hole and the self-centring pilot drill used to drill one pilot hole in each hinge. The screw is driven home and the door checked for fit, adjustments made, and the remaining holes drilled and screws driven. Recesses are cut for the finger pulls on the doors by the same method as for the recessed drawer pulls. Brass double ball catches are fitted – and the spring loading on the balls is adjusted to get a satisfying 'clunk'.

Routing waste from dovetails

Brass fittings

The recessed drawer handles, finger pulls, straps and corners, used on the original piece were standard military chest fittings and still available from H E Savill.

The raised head brass screws came from Screwfix.

H E Savill 7 to 12 St Martins Place, Scarborough, N Yorks YO11 2QH
Tel: 01723 373032

Screwfix Direct FREEPOST, Yeovil BA22
Tel: 0500 414141 Fax: 0800 056 2256
Email: sales@screwfix.com

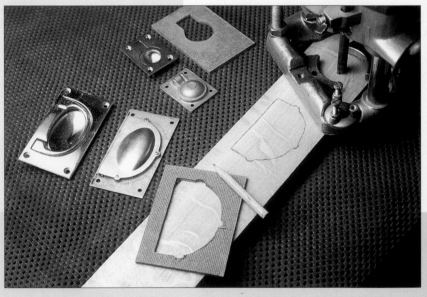

Templates and marked out recess for handles

hand-planing and sanding to a minimum. They are then finished, a groove is cut on the inside edges of the rails and stiles to take the fielded panels, and the inside edges of the frames are finished.

The doors are assembled, glued and clamped, checked for square and wind, and left to set.

Finish

My client had specified a tough, totally matt, maintenance-free finish. I remembered using matt polyurethane on the previous piece so elected for the same on this one. I stirred it thoroughly – which is very important when using a matt finish or it will 'gloss up' – unevenly!

Give it three coats, leaving 24 hours between coats, and cutting back with 320 grit aluminium oxide paper between them. Do not use wire wool on oak as any tiny pieces left in the wood will react with the acid in the wood and turn black. I hesitated to use more than three coats as a slight gloss begins to form, the more coats that are applied.

After the finish has thoroughly hardened, the brassware is fitted. It was all pre-polished and lacquered, and the screws are brass and slotted rather than Posidrive, so great care was taken with the electric screwdriver! I pre-drilled all

the holes with a 2mm drill and used a small 2.4v powerdriver with a nice slow speed, held steady with both hands. All the screw slots are lined up horizontally, of course!

Conclusion

I enjoyed this bit of detective work and felt that the result is a passable copy of the original. I love working in oak and particularly like this mixture of natural oak and brass – it gives a nice simple, solid, English-looking piece – and the client was pleased. ■

Corner storage

How to go about making a corner cupboard

SOON AFTER I began writing articles, I discovered that I was in need of extra storage space in my study, to keep all the bits and pieces of photographic equipment that I had acquired in the process of taking photographs for my articles. With only limited space available, I decided to make a hanging corner cupboard which would fit neatly in the space between a bookshelf and a tall chest. As a rule, corner cupboards don't provide as much space as they appear to, because the shape of the shelves restricts the storage possibilities – but in this case it wasn't a problem as all the items I wanted to keep in it were small.

Design

When I make furniture for myself I use it as an opportunity to try something new or different, so that I'm learning as I go, and expanding my range. The centre piece in my study is a large partner's desk, in fumed oak with sycamore drawer fronts and panels. Apart from fulfilling its function extremely well, it has been successful as a piece of display furniture which has generated at least a dozen major pieces of commissioned work. I did not have an example of a corner cupboard, so this was a useful addition. I decided that I would continue the theme of the desk, and go for sycamore, or fumed oak, or a mix – depending on what offcuts I could find in the workshop!

Timber selection

Timber selection is a bit of a grand term in this case as I had decided to use offcuts – in the event there was not enough oak (*Quercus robur*) and I used sweet chestnut (*Castanea sativa*) for the sides and shelves. Sweet chestnut fumes to the same colour as oak, and is almost indistinguishable in appearance. It is softer and probably a little easier to work. It is also cheaper!

I found a suitable piece of nicely figured sycamore (*Acer pseudo-platanus*) thick enough to split through and rejoin as a book-matched panel for the door. I even found a spare sycamore door pull. It was with some satisfaction that I gathered the 'free' materials for the cupboard.

"I decided that I would go for sycamore, or fumed oak, or a mix – depending on what offcuts I could find in the workshop!"

ABOVE LEFT:
Good use of space –
a cupboard for
storing small things

> "Sycamore reacts to the fuming process by going a very unattractive dirty grey and must therefore be kept out of the fuming tent"

I chose the best faces of the sides, top, and base, for the inside of the cupboard, as the other faces would not be seen in normal use. Of course the best face of the fronts is used for the outside.

Carcass Construction

The sides and shelves are cut to size, the front edges of the shelves are rounded over, and the shoulders cut in where they fit in to the fronts, see drawing. The edge of the fronts which fit the door are cut to 22½° and the tops shouldered. The housings are cut in the fronts and right hand side, and all these pieces are finished at this point, before assembly.

Next, the top and base are cut to size and shape, and the housings for the fronts and sides cut 13mm (½in) in from the edge. The front edges are rounded over, and both pieces finished on the inside.

Assembly

The entire cabinet is now dry assembled to check the fit of all joints, and any necessary adjustments made. Assembly is in two stages – first, PVA glue is applied to the housings in the fronts and sides, and then the fronts, sides, and shelves are fitted together. To help keep the whole thing true, fit the top and base on dry, fit the clamps from front to back, check for square, and leave to set.

When this is dry, apply PVA to the top and base housings, fit them to the sides and fronts, and clamp from top to base. Again, check all is square, and leave to set.

Door

The door is a standard frame and front fielded panel construction. The frame is oak, 50mm by 19mm (2in by ¾in) thick. The panel is contrasting sycamore and has to be removable as

ABOVE: Close-up of top left of front – showing decorative strip, top overhang, rounded edge, door frame and sycamore fielded panel

Preparation

First, draw the outline of the top and base to real size on hardboard. The sides and fronts are housed directly into the top and base allowing a 13mm (½in) overhang. The sides fit into the fronts in 6mm by 16mm (¼in by ⅝in) housings, and the left-hand side fits to the right hand side, at the back, in another 6mm by 16mm (1¼in by ⅝in) housing. The door side of the fronts is drawn at an angle of 22½°. The shelves are let in to the sides in 6mm by 16mm (¼in by ⅝in) housings.

Drawing this all to size on the hardboard allows accurate measurements to be taken for all the component parts. I also made a full size pattern for the shelves from the same drawing.

Next, the carcass timber is faced and thicknessed to 16mm (⅝in) and, where necessary, jointed to width. The hardboard patterns are used to mark the triangular pieces out economically. The grain direction of the shelves, top, and base, should be parallel to the line of the front to allow for movement when jointed to the sides – although I admit to taking some liberties here as I was a bit tight on materials, and I knew from experience that my workshop humidity level was similar to that of my house. Happily there was no subsequent problem. I would not have done this with a client's piece because, apart from the risk of movement, it looks better with the grain running parallel to the front line.

RIGHT: Cupboard open, showing shelves and inside

> "I chose the best faces of the sides, top, and base for the inside of the cupboard, as the other faces would not be seen in normal use"

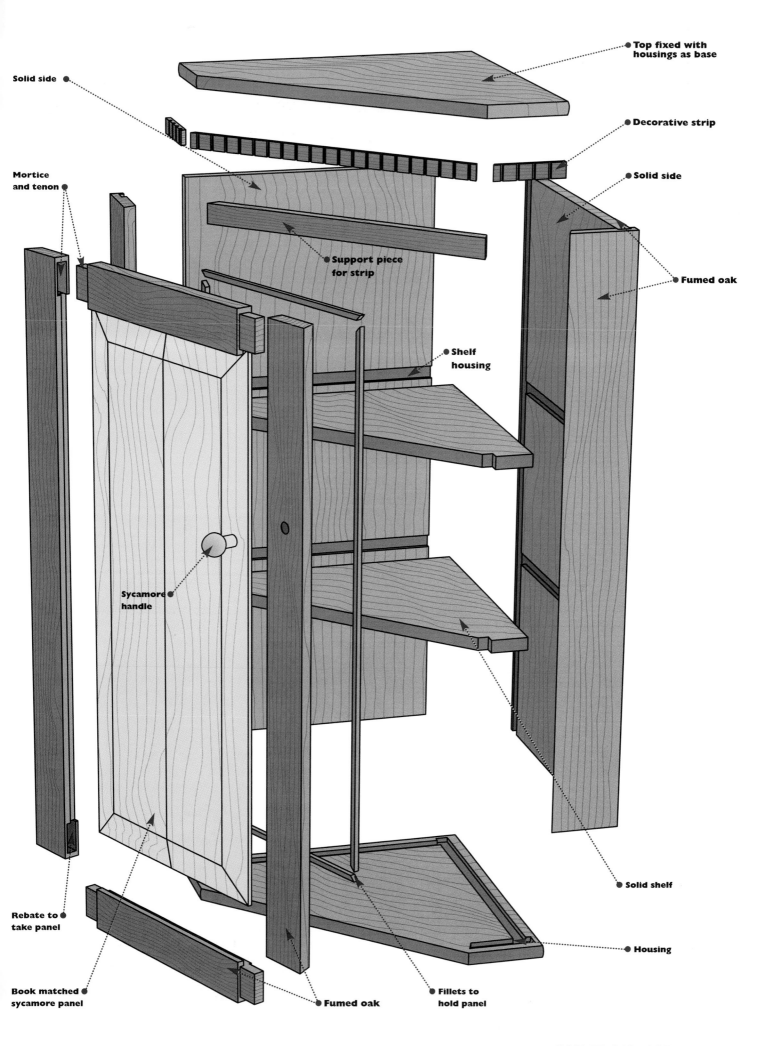

Solid side

Mortice
and tenon

Rebate to
take panel

Book matched
sycamore panel

Sycamore
handle

Fumed oak

Fillets to
hold panel

Top fixed with
housings as base

Decorative strip

Solid side

Fumed oak

Support piece
for strip

Shelf
housing

Solid shelf

Housing

RIGHT: APTC
hinge siting
pre-drill, being
used to fit
door

FAR RIGHT:
Decorative
strip being cut
on radial arm
saw, showing
register mark

"The grain direction of the shelves, top, and base, should be parallel to the line of the front to allow for movement when jointed to the sides"

it has a different finish. Sycamore reacts to the fuming process by going a very unattractive dirty grey and must therefore be kept out of the fuming tent.

The frame pieces are cut to size, morticed and tenoned, and rebated to take the panel. Enough meat is left on the outside edges of the uprights to allow for planing to 22½° to match the internal edges of the fronts. Some strips of oak are also cut to size, with a mitred corner, to retain the panel when fitted.

The panel is made up from a figured piece of sycamore split in two, through its thickness, and joined as a book-match panel. The raised panel is marked out with a 3mm (⅛in) deep groove on the edge of the fielding on

the table saw, and the majority of the waste for the fielded edge removed with a router. The fielding is then finished with a sharp plane and sanded. The panel is placed in the frame and the retaining strips adjusted to fit. These strips are pinned loosely into place to hold the panel while the door is fitted. Incidentally, always pre-drill holes just under the diameter of the pin in such strips – it holds the pin in position for the hammer and prevents splitting the strip.

Fitting the door

The outside edges of the door are planed to 22½° to match the edges on the fronts. Do not be tempted to cut the fronts of the cupboard to 45° and

leave the door edges square for ease of fitting – there will not be enough thickness left on the cupboard fronts to take the hinge screws. Believe me – I've tried it!

I had a pair of flush-fitting electro-plated brass hinges lying around so I decided to use them for their ease, and to see how they looked. They save little time, and when fitted, are not strong, and look cheap, which of course they are – I won't use them again! For the door, I used an electro-brassed magnetic catch, which I found slimmer and better looking than the brown or white plastic variety. These are not cheap, however, and I still prefer a brass ball catch for its looks.

To drill the screw holes for the hinges I used the APTC hinge siting pre-drill and found it very good, *see photo*. Essentially, it is a spring-loaded outer sleeve, fitted round the drill, which locates in the counter sinking on the hinge, and centres the drill in the hole. It worked well and was a good buy for a couple of quid – drilling depth was critical because of the angled edges. I marked the depth on the drill with a piece of sticky tape to avoid drilling through. I drilled for the sycamore door pull and dry fitted it, then removed it, and the sycamore panel, ready to fume the oak.

Fuming

I made a temporary fuming tent from polythene sheet and string, the edges held down with battens of scrap.

The cupboard is wiped over with white spirit to highlight any defects or glue marks, and carefully finished – sanding after fuming will leave marks. It is then placed in the tent on its side, resting on some pointed dowels let into pieces of scrap. This supports it on a face which would not be seen, and leaves virtually no marks anyway. .880 ammonia is poured into some

DECORATIVE STRIP

I decided to add a small decorative strip to the top of the cupboard, and in order to support it, needed to add a cross piece under the front of the top. This is cut to size, with a 22½° butt joint at each end, to fit to the inner edges of the fronts, and glued and clamped to the top.

A saw cut 3mm (⅛in) deep is cut every 19mm (¾in) in a strip of oak 19mm by 6mm (¾in by ¼in), to leave a series of small raised pieces to form the decorative strip. Mark the first cut and, using a register pencil, mark on the fence of the radial arm saw, and make the remaining cuts, *see photo*. A similar result could be achieved, albeit more slowly, by marking each cut and making the cut by hand, using a tenon saw with a wide set and a depth-stop clamped to the blade.

The strip is sanded and finished, and the centre piece cut to size, with a 22½° butt join face at each end, and glued to the cross strip. The two side pieces are then cut, fitted, and glued to the fronts of the cupboard. The join between the sides and the front of the strip should be in the same position on the raised decorative square, on each side, or it will look unbalanced.

"When I make furniture for myself I use it as an opportunity to try something new or different"

368

13

95

Grain direction for top, base, shelves

19

Decorative strip

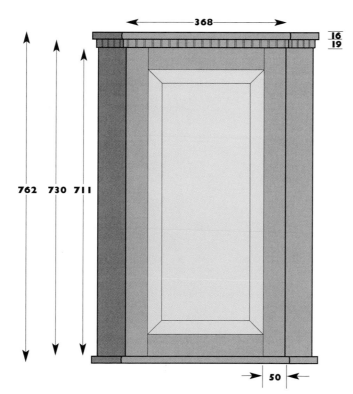

368

16
19

762 730 711

50

"Drawing all the pieces to size on hardboard allows accurate measurements to be taken for all the component parts"

saucers, placed inside the tent and the whole thing left overnight. The usual precautions must be taken with the ammonia, the most important being eye protection. Ammonia is extremely dangerous to the eyes and damage can be permanent – particularly relevant in my case!

Finish
Once the oak is fumed give it three coats of Danish oil, leaving 24 hours and lightly rubbing down, between

coats. Sycamore yellows when treated with Danish oil and I wanted to keep its creamy-white look, so I used a water-based acrylic varnish with a UV filter on the panel and door pull. The panel and pull are fitted and the whole thing given two coats of wax and buffed to a nice sheen.

Conclusion
I was pleased with the result, it cost very little in time or materials, and

holds all the small kit it was intended for. When we moved recently, there was a suitable corner in the study of the new house, just waiting for it. ▪

Supplier: APTC hinge siting pre-drills come in three sizes: 5/64 in, 7/64 in, 9/64 in from **Axminster Power Tool Centre,** *Chard Street, Axminster, Devon, EX13 5DZ, tel 01297 33656 fax 01297 35242*

Apothecary's chest

It's a calculated risk working with burr elm

I LOVE THE challenge of working in burr elm (*Ulmus procera*). There is an element of risk, and as with certain other potential objects of beauty, the desired result can only be achieved with a careful approach!

I have made several of these chests using various contrasting woods for the carcass, and up to fourteen drawers with burr fronts, but this speculative piece made for a museum, *see panel*, is the first in solid burr throughout.

Design

This piece is loosely based on the apothecary's chest of pre-NHS times; the stylised drawer attachment both adapts its function and improves balance and interest.

It also makes use of the availability of small pieces of burr, and gives me the welcome opportunity to make plenty of drawers.

Making panels

Time and care spent marking out and making the panels has a profound effect on the end result. The distinctive grain pattern of the burr makes joins difficult if a patchwork quilt appearance is to be avoided.

Try to book-match sequential boards, or mask the join by flowing the grain and colour through it. Blemishes can be put on the inside or made into a feature!

Before gluing up, cut the pieces over-size, mark them carefully, and lay them out to see how they relate to each other.

The top and drawer fronts should have the best figure. While each will be a picture in its own right, it must relate to the whole to give an overall pleasing effect.

If, as a result of the wild grain, there is end-grain along the joints, strengthen them with a loose tongue.

Drawer frames

Burr tends to move more than most other woods, so allowances must be made for this in the construction.

The main movement is across the grain, and as the grain in the top, sides and base is more or less running in the same direction, there should be little problem. The drawer rails, however, run across the grain.

> "The distinctive grain pattern of the burr makes joins difficult"

ABOVE: Careful matching of boards for the top and drawer fronts

ABOVE LEFT AND RIGHT: Cramping up has to be done in sequence

"Allow plenty of time – in the words of David Savage this is not a Friday afternoon job"

Do not glue the mortise and tenons at the back of the frame; leave a 3mm ($^1/_8$in) gap to allow for expansion and contraction.

Make the frames 1mm ($^3/_{64}$in) wider at the back than the front to allow for easy drawer movement. For the same reason the drawer spacers should be tapered front to back by 1.5mm ($^1/_{16}$in) each side; fit them very carefully, and cut the mortises for the front uprights between the drawers.

Construction

Cut the sides to size, and slot to receive the frames and back. Do as much of the final filling and finishing as possible before assembly.

The first stage in the assembly of the carcass is probably the most difficult as the drawer frames must be glued into the sides, and the uprights between the rails, at the same time.

Only the front and back rail ends should be glued into the side slots, to enable the dry joint at the back to run smoothly.

Do a trial dry assembly to check everything, prepare the clamps and equipment, and above all allow plenty of time. In the words of David Savage this is not "a Friday afternoon job".

Check the diagonals back and front to ensure all is square; leave to set. Indulgence in a little cheating allows fitting the uprights first, using a plugged screw with which to pull up the joint, then fitting the frames to the sides.

ABOVE: Drawer detail

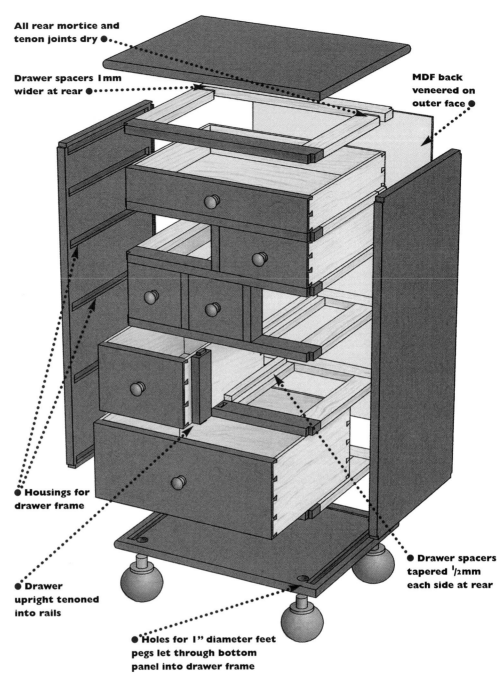

All rear mortice and tenon joints dry ●····

Drawer spacers 1mm wider at rear ● ·········

MDF back veneered on outer face ●

● Housings for drawer frame

● Drawer spacers tapered ½mm each side at rear

● Drawer upright tenoned into rails

● Holes for 1" diameter feet pegs let through bottom panel into drawer frame

Top, base, back

Cut the top, base and back to size, allowing the extra 1mm width at the back; slot the top and base to receive the sides and back.

I use suitably faced 5mm MDF for the back, and glue it in all round for extra strength.

Rounding over the edges of the top and bottom protects them from chipping and provides a nice highlight to the finish.

Clamp up, check for square and leave to set.

Drawers

The drawers are constructed in the normal way. I always use cedar of Lebanon (*Cedrus libani*) for the linings, and cedar-faced MDF glued in all round for the bases, again for extra strength.

The smell of cedar is wonderful, it repels insects – and attracts customers!

When preparing the drawer fronts keep them a tight, tapered fit to allow for adjustment when fitting; finishing the inside faces at this stage is easier than doing it when the drawers are assembled.

When dovetailing the fronts, keep tools razor-sharp and pressure-light; the wild grain entails cutting both with and against it, and the work is all too easily chipped. As a last resort keep the Superglue handy!

Fit the drawers a little looser than usual; to minimise any visual effect with the shadow line, set them back about 1mm from the front.

"The old oil adage of 'once a day for a week, once a week for a month and once a year thereafter' is not far out"

Knobs, feet

Taking advantage of more odd lumps of leftover burr, I chose bun feet, adopting a similar shape for the knobs. Again, the rounded surfaces show off the oiled finish nicely.

The pegs which fit the knobs and feet are better made as loose dowels from a suitable straight-grained timber, and glued in. If turned from solid burr with an unkind grain they can snap.

Finishing

A Danish-oiled finish is the best choice; it brings out the deep richness of the grain pattern and colour, and is improved with time and tender loving care. The burr can be quite porous, and oil penetrates well into the wood, helping to stabilise it.

The old oil adage of 'once a day for a week, once a week for a month and once a year thereafter' is not far out.

ABOVE: Sharp tools and care are needed to avoid chipping the burr

The first coat is liberally applied, left to soak in, and refreshed every 15 to 20 minutes until it will take no more – four to six coats. Wipe it off with a soft cloth, allowing no oil to build up on the surface, and leave it to harden for 24 hours in a warmish, dry place.

The surface is cut back with a Scotchbrite grey pad, and further light coats applied every 24 hours until the desired effect is achieved.

Ensuring that there is no build up of oil on the surface, the last coat can be cut back and buffed with a soft cloth, or waxed and buffed.

Future care amounts to an annual light coat of teak oil.

The inside surfaces of the burr should also be oiled in a similar way, but not those in contact with the moving surfaces of the drawers; these should be sealed by a thorough waxing.

Stunning impact

The inherent instability of burr may mean a slight sacrifice of engineering tolerances, but this minus is far outweighed by the plus of its stunning visual impact.

Close tolerances do not necessarily feed the soul, but the beauty of this wood does. A piece of burr furniture lives, it has visual – and actual – movement, and is lent a natural beauty by virtue of its instability.

Burr makes a fitting tribute to our devastated elm trees, so good luck to those who venture a piece in this lovely timber. ∎

RIGHT: Feet and knobs are turned

Metric/Imperial Conversion Chart

mm	inch	mm	inch	mm	inch	mm	inch
1	0.03937	27	1.06299	80	3.14960	340	13.38582
2	0.07874	28	1.10236	90	3.54330	350	13.77952
3	0.11811	29	1.14173	100	3.93700		
4	0.15748	30	1.18110			360	14.17322
5	0.19685			110	4.33070	370	14.56692
		31	1.22047	120	4.72440	380	14.96063
6	0.23622	32	1.25984	130	5.11811	390	15.35433
7	0.27559	33	1.29921	140	5.51181	400	15.74803
8	0.31496	34	1.33858	150	5.90551		
9	0.35433	35	1.37795			410	16.14173
10	0.39370			160	6.29921	420	16.53543
		36	1.41732	170	6.69291	430	16.92913
11	0.43307	37	1.45669	180	7.08661	440	17.32283
12	0.47244	38	1.49606	190	7.48031	450	17.71653
13	0.51181	39	1.53543	200	7.87401		
14	0.55118	40	1.57480			460	18.11023
15	0.59055			210	8.26771	470	18.50393
		41	1.61417	220	8.66141	480	18.89763
16	0.62992	42	1.65354	230	9.05511	490	19.29133
17	0.66929	43	1.69291	240	9.44881	500	19.68504
18	0.70866	44	1.73228	250	9.84252		
19	0.74803	45	1.77165				
20	0.78740			260	10.23622		
		46	1.81102	270	10.62992		
21	0.82677	47	1.85039	280	11.02362		
22	0.86614	48	1.88976	290	11.41732		
23	0.90551	49	1.92913	300	11.81102		
24	0.94488	50	1.96850	310	12.20472		
25	0.98425	60	2.36220	320	12.59842		
26	1.02362	70	2.75590	330	12.99212		

1 mm = 0.03937 inch
1 cm = 0.3937 inch
1 m = 3.281 feet
1 inch = 25.4 mm
1 foot = 304.8 mm
1 yard = 914.4 mm

Imperial/Metric Conversion Chart

inch		mm	inch		mm	inch		mm
0	0	0	23/64	0.359375	9.1281	45/64	0.703125	17.8594
1/64	0.015625	0.3969				23/32	0.71875	18.2562
1/32	0.03125	0.7938	3/8	0.375	9.5250	47/64	0.734375	18.6531
3/64	0.046875	1.1906	25/64	0.390625	9.9219			
1/16	0.0625	1.5875	13/32	0.40625	10.3188	3/4	0.750	19.0500
			27/64	0.421875	10.7156			
5/64	0.078125	1.9844				49/64	0.765625	19.4469
3/32	0.09375	2.3812	7/16	0.4375	11.1125	25/32	0.78125	19.8438
7/64	0.109375	2.7781	29/64	0.453125	11.5094	51/64	0.796875	20.2406
			15/32	0.46875	11.9062	13/16	0.8125	20.6375
1/8	0.125	3.1750	31/64	0.484375	12.3031			
9/64	0.140625	3.5719				53/64	0.828125	21.0344
5/32	0.15625	3.9688	1/2	0.500	12.700	27/32	0.84375	21.4312
11/64	0.171875	4.3656	33/64	0.515625	13.0969	55/64	0.858375	21.8281
			17/32	0.53125	13.4938			
3/16	0.1875	4.7625	35/64	0.546875	13.8906	7/8	0.875	22.2250
13/64	0.203125	5.1594	9/16	0.5625	14.2875	57/64	0.890625	22.6219
7/32	0.21875	5.5562				29/32	0.90625	23.0188
15/64	0.234375	5.9531	37/64	0.578125	14.6844	59/64	0.921875	23.4156
1/4	0.250	6.3500	19/32	0.59375	15.0812			
			39/64	0.609375	15.4781	15/16	0.9375	23.8125
17/64	0.265625	6.7469				61/64	0.953125	24.2094
9/32	0.28125	7.1438	5/8	0.625	15.8750	31/32	0.96875	24.6062
19/64	0.296875	7.5406	41/64	0.640625	16.2719	63/64	0.984375	25.0031
5/16	0.3125	7.9375	21/32	0.65625	16.6688			
			43/64	0.671875	17.0656			
21/64	0.1328125	8.3344						
11/32	0.34375	8.7312	11/16	0.6875	17.4625	1 inch = 1.000 = 25.40 mm		

ACKNOWLEDGEMENTS

Turning the raw material which I supply into the superbly presented articles in *F&C* magazine is achieved by the hard work, charm, courage, humility, unarmed combat skills and psychological warfare proficiency, of all the staff at GMC. They are all a pleasure to deal with, from Jill who womans the phones – delightfully, to Paul who emperors the universe – masterfully.

I'd like to thank them all individually – Alan Phillips for the money, Paul Richardson for getting me started and guiding me along the way, Colin Eden-Eadon, Andrea Hargreaves and Liz McClair for judicious editing, Simon Rodway and Ian Hall for their brilliant illustrations, and Jill for her pleasant greetings.

For turning the articles into a book many thanks to Stephanie Horner for her help, encouragement and professional judgement at a difficult time, Kylie Johnston for her advice and editing skills, and Chris Skarbon for his sound advice not to take up modelling, and the superb results after a long, cold day's photography.

Most of all thanks to my wife Yvonne for her help and encouragement, for bringing a new aspect to my furniture designs in particular and to life in general, lending me her hands and other assistance with the photographs, and for just putting up with me.

Wardrobe selection by Chris Skarbon.

Hairstyle by Mandy, manicure by Anita of 'Soap Opera'.

ABOUT THE AUTHOR

Kevin Ley lives with his artist and teacher wife Yvonne in their picturesque cottage in a South Shropshire wooded nature reserve.

Kevin divides his time between making furniture in the workshop next to the house, writing and photographing pieces for the GMC woodworking magazines, and obeying the whims, wishes and commands of Yvonne as they 'collaborate' on the improvements to their cottage and large garden.

They both enjoy fast cars, reading, talking, music, sampling the delights of the local eating and watering holes, keeping fit – and being bossy.

INDEX

TITLES AVAILABLE FROM
GMC Publications
BOOKS

WOODCARVING

The Art of the Woodcarver	GMC Publications
Carving Architectural Detail in Wood: The Classical Tradition	Frederick Wilbur
Carving Birds & Beasts	GMC Publications
Carving the Human Figure: Studies in Wood and Stone	Dick Onians
Carving Nature: Wildlife Studies in Wood	Frank Fox-Wilson
Carving Realistic Birds	David Tippey
Decorative Woodcarving	Jeremy Williams
Elements of Woodcarving	Chris Pye
Essential Woodcarving Techniques	Dick Onians
Further Useful Tips for Woodcarvers	GMC Publications
Lettercarving in Wood: A Practical Course	Chris Pye
Making & Using Working Drawings for Realistic Model Animals	
	Basil F. Fordham
Power Tools for Woodcarving	David Tippey
Practical Tips for Turners & Carvers	GMC Publications
Relief Carving in Wood: A Practical Introduction	Chris Pye
Understanding Woodcarving	GMC Publications
Understanding Woodcarving in the Round	GMC Publications
Useful Techniques for Woodcarvers	GMC Publications
Wildfowl Carving – Volume 1	Jim Pearce
Wildfowl Carving – Volume 2	Jim Pearce
Woodcarving: A Complete Course	Ron Butterfield
Woodcarving: A Foundation Course	Zoë Gertner
Woodcarving for Beginners	GMC Publications
Woodcarving Tools & Equipment Test Reports	GMC Publications
Woodcarving Tools, Materials & Equipment	Chris Pye

WOODTURNING

Adventures in Woodturning	David Springett
Bert Marsh: Woodturner	Bert Marsh
Bowl Turning Techniques Masterclass	Tony Boase
Colouring Techniques for Woodturners	Jan Sanders
Contemporary Turned Wood: New Perspectives in a Rich Tradition	
	Ray Leier, Jan Peters & Kevin Wallace
The Craftsman Woodturner	Peter Child
Decorative Techniques for Woodturners	Hilary Bowen
Fun at the Lathe	R.C. Bell
Illustrated Woodturning Techniques	John Hunnex
Intermediate Woodturning Projects	GMC Publications
Keith Rowley's Woodturning Projects	Keith Rowley
Practical Tips for Turners & Carvers	GMC Publications
Turning Green Wood	Michael O'Donnell
Turning Miniatures in Wood	John Sainsbury
Turning Pens and Pencils	Kip Christensen & Rex Burningham
Understanding Woodturning	Ann & Bob Phillips
Useful Techniques for Woodturners	GMC Publications
Useful Woodturning Projects	GMC Publications
Woodturning: Bowls, Platters, Hollow Forms, Vases, Vessels, Bottles, Flasks, Tankards, Plates	GMC Publications
Woodturning: A Foundation Course (New Edition)	Keith Rowley
Woodturning: A Fresh Approach	Robert Chapman
Woodturning: An Individual Approach	Dave Regester
Woodturning: A Source Book of Shapes	John Hunnex
Woodturning Jewellery	Hilary Bowen
Woodturning Masterclass	Tony Boase
Woodturning Techniques	GMC Publications
Woodturning Tools & Equipment Test Reports	GMC Publications
Woodturning Wizardry	David Springett

WOODWORKING

Advanced Scrollsaw Projects	GMC Publications
Bird Boxes and Feeders for the Garden	Dave Mackenzie
Complete Woodfinishing	Ian Hosker
David Charlesworth's Furniture-Making Techniques	David Charlesworth
The Encyclopedia of Joint Making	Terrie Noll
Furniture & Cabinetmaking Projects	GMC Publications
Furniture-Making Projects for the Wood Craftsman	GMC Publications
Furniture-Making Techniques for the Wood Craftsman	GMC Publications
Furniture Projects	Rod Wales
Furniture Restoration (Practical Crafts)	Kevin Jan Bonner
Furniture Restoration and Repair for Beginners	Kevin Jan Bonner

Furniture Restoration Workshop	Kevin Jan Bonner
Green Woodwork	Mike Abbott
Kevin Ley's Furniture Projects	Kevin Ley
Making & Modifying Woodworking Tools	Jim Kingshott
Making Chairs and Tables	GMC Publications
Making Classic English Furniture	Paul Richardson
Making Little Boxes from Wood	John Bennett
Making Screw Threads in Wood	Fred Holder
Making Shaker Furniture	Barry Jackson
Making Woodwork Aids and Devices	Robert Wearing
Mastering the Router	Ron Fox
Minidrill: Fifteen Projects	John Everett
Pine Furniture Projects for the Home	Dave Mackenzie
Practical Scrollsaw Patterns	John Everett
Router Magic: Jigs, Fixtures and Tricks to Unleash your Router's Full Potential	Bill Hylton
Routing for Beginners	Anthony Bailey
The Scrollsaw: Twenty Projects	John Everett
Sharpening: The Complete Guide	Jim Kingshott
Sharpening Pocket Reference Book	Jim Kingshott
Simple Scrollsaw Projects	GMC Publications
Space-Saving Furniture Projects	Dave Mackenzie
Stickmaking: A Complete Course	Andrew Jones & Clive George
Stickmaking Handbook	Andrew Jones & Clive George
Test Reports: The Router and Furniture & Cabinetmaking	GMC Publications
Veneering: A Complete Course	Ian Hosker
Veneering Handbook	Ian Hosker
Woodfinishing Handbook (Practical Crafts)	Ian Hosker
Woodworking with the Router: Professional Router Techniques any Woodworker can Use	Bill Hylton & Fred Matlack
The Workshop	Jim Kingshott

UPHOLSTERY

The Upholsterer's Pocket Reference Book	David James
Upholstery: A Complete Course (Revised Edition)	David James
Upholstery Restoration	David James
Upholstery Techniques & Projects	David James
Upholstery Tips and Hints	David James

TOYMAKING

Designing & Making Wooden Toys	Terry Kelly
Fun to Make Wooden Toys & Games	Jeff & Jennie Loader
Restoring Rocking Horses	Clive Green & Anthony Dew
Scrollsaw Toy Projects	Ivor Carlyle
Scrollsaw Toys for All Ages	Ivor Carlyle
Wooden Toy Projects	GMC Publications

DOLLS' HOUSES AND MINIATURES

1/12 Scale Character Figures for the Dolls' House	James Carrington
Architecture for Dolls' Houses	Joyce Percival
The Authentic Georgian Dolls' House	Brian Long
A Beginners' Guide to the Dolls' House Hobby	Jean Nisbett
Celtic, Medieval and Tudor Wall Hangings in 1/12 Scale Needlepoint	Sandra Whitehead
The Complete Dolls' House Book	Jean Nisbett
The Dolls' House 1/24 Scale: A Complete Introduction	Jean Nisbett
Dolls' House Accessories, Fixtures and Fittings	Andrea Barham
Dolls' House Bathrooms: Lots of Little Loos	Patricia King
Dolls' House Fireplaces and Stoves	Patricia King
Dolls' House Window Treatments	Eve Harwood
Easy to Make Dolls' House Accessories	Andrea Barham
Heraldic Miniature Knights	Peter Greenhill
How to Make Your Dolls' House Special: Fresh Ideas for Decorating	Beryl Armstrong
Make Your Own Dolls' House Furniture	Maurice Harper
Making Dolls' House Furniture	Patricia King
Making Georgian Dolls' Houses	Derek Rowbottom
Making Miniature Food and Market Stalls	Angie Scarr
Making Miniature Gardens	Freida Gray
Making Miniature Oriental Rugs & Carpets	Meik & Ian McNaughton

Making Period Dolls' House Accessories — *Andrea Barham*
Making Tudor Dolls' Houses — *Derek Rowbottom*
Making Victorian Dolls' House Furniture — *Patricia King*
Miniature Bobbin Lace — *Roz Snowden*
Miniature Embroidery for the Georgian Dolls' House — *Pamela Warner*
Miniature Embroidery for the Victorian Dolls' House — *Pamela Warner*
Miniature Needlepoint Carpets — *Janet Granger*
More Miniature Oriental Rugs & Carpets — *Meik & Ian McNaughton*
Needlepoint 1/12 Scale: Design Collections for the Dolls' House — *Felicity Price*
The Secrets of the Dolls' House Makers — *Jean Nisbett*

CRAFTS

American Patchwork Designs in Needlepoint — *Melanie Tacon*
A Beginners' Guide to Rubber Stamping — *Brenda Hunt*
Blackwork: A New Approach — *Brenda Day*
Celtic Cross Stitch Designs — *Carol Phillipson*
Celtic Knotwork Designs — *Sheila Sturrock*
Celtic Knotwork Handbook — *Sheila Sturrock*
Celtic Spirals and Other Designs — *Sheila Sturrock*
Collage from Seeds, Leaves and Flowers — *Joan Carver*
Complete Pyrography — *Stephen Poole*
Contemporary Smocking — *Dorothea Hall*
Creating Colour with Dylon — *Dylon International*
Creative Doughcraft — *Patricia Hughes*
Creative Embroidery Techniques Using Colour Through Gold — *Daphne J. Ashby & Jackie Woolsey*
The Creative Quilter: Techniques and Projects — *Pauline Brown*
Decorative Beaded Purses — *Enid Taylor*
Designing and Making Cards — *Glennis Gilruth*
Glass Engraving Pattern Book — *John Everett*
Glass Painting — *Emma Sedman*
Handcrafted Rugs — *Sandra Hardy*
How to Arrange Flowers: A Japanese Approach to English Design — *Taeko Marvelly*
How to Make First-Class Cards — *Debbie Brown*
An Introduction to Crewel Embroidery — *Mave Glenny*
Making and Using Working Drawings for Realistic Model Animals — *Basil F. Fordham*
Making Character Bears — *Valerie Tyler*
Making Decorative Screens — *Amanda Howes*
Making Fairies and Fantastical Creatures — *Julie Sharp*
Making Greetings Cards for Beginners — *Pat Sutherland*
Making Hand-Sewn Boxes: Techniques and Projects — *Jackie Woolsey*
Making Knitwear Fit — *Pat Ashforth & Steve Plummer*
Making Mini Cards, Gift Tags & Invitations — *Glennis Gilruth*
Making Soft-Bodied Dough Characters — *Patricia Hughes*
Natural Ideas for Christmas: Fantastic Decorations to Make — *Josie Cameron-Ashcroft & Carol Cox*
Needlepoint: A Foundation Course — *Sandra Hardy*
New Ideas for Crochet: Stylish Projects for the Home — *Darsha Capaldi*
Patchwork for Beginners — *Pauline Brown*
Pyrography Designs — *Norma Gregory*
Pyrography Handbook (Practical Crafts) — *Stephen Poole*
Ribbons and Roses — *Lee Lockheed*
Rose Windows for Quilters — *Angela Besley*
Rubber Stamping with Other Crafts — *Lynne Garner*
Sponge Painting — *Ann Rooney*
Stained Glass: Techniques and Projects — *Mary Shanahan*
Step-by-Step Pyrography Projects for the Solid Point Machine — *Norma Gregory*
Tassel Making for Beginners — *Enid Taylor*
Tatting Collage — *Lindsay Rogers*
Temari: A Traditional Japanese Embroidery Technique — *Margaret Ludlow*
Theatre Models in Paper and Card — *Robert Burgess*
Trip Around the World: 25 Patchwork, Quilting and Appliqué Projects — *Gail Lawther*
Trompe l'Oeil: Techniques and Projects — *Jan Lee Johnson*
Wool Embroidery and Design — *Lee Lockheed*

GARDENING

Auriculas for Everyone: How to Grow and Show Perfect Plants — *Mary Robinson*
Beginners' Guide to Herb Gardening — *Yvonne Cuthbertson*
Bird Boxes and Feeders for the Garden — *Dave Mackenzie*
The Birdwatcher's Garden — *Hazel & Pamela Johnson*
Broad-Leaved Evergreens — *Stephen G. Haw*
Companions to Clematis: Growing Clematis with Other Plants — *Marigold Badcock*
Creating Contrast with Dark Plants — *Freya Martin*
Creating Small Habitats for Wildlife in your Garden — *Josie Briggs*
Gardening with Wild Plants — *Julian Slatcher*
Growing Cacti and Other Succulents in the Conservatory and Indoors — *Shirley-Anne Bell*
Growing Cacti and Other Succulents in the Garden — *Shirley Anne Bell*
Hardy Perennials: A Beginner's Guide — *Eric Sawford*

The Living Tropical Greenhouse: Creating a Haven for Butterflies — *John & Maureen Tampion*
Orchids are Easy: A Beginner's Guide to their Care and Cultivation — *Tom Gilland*
Plant Alert: A Garden Guide for Parents — *Catherine Collins*
Planting Plans for Your Garden — *Jenny Shukman*
Plants that Span the Seasons — *Roger Wilson*
Sink and Container Gardening Using Dwarf Hardy Plants — *Chris & Valerie Wheeler*

PHOTOGRAPHY

An Essential Guide to Bird Photography — *Steve Young*
Light in the Landscape: A Photographer's Year — *Peter Watson*

VIDEOS

Drop-in and Pinstuffed Seats — *David James*
Stuffover Upholstery — *David James*
Elliptical Turning — *David Springett*
Woodturning Wizardry — *David Springett*
Turning Between Centres: The Basics — *Dennis White*
Turning Bowls — *Dennis White*
Boxes, Goblets and Screw Threads — *Dennis White*
Novelties and Projects — *Dennis White*
Classic Profiles — *Dennis White*
Twists and Advanced Turning — *Dennis White*
Sharpening the Professional Way — *Jim Kingshott*
Sharpening Turning & Carving Tools — *Jim Kingshott*
Bowl Turning — *John Jordan*
Hollow Turning — *John Jordan*
Woodturning: A Foundation Course — *Keith Rowley*
Carving a Figure: The Female Form — *Ray Gonzalez*
The Router: A Beginner's Guide — *Alan Goodsell*
The Scroll Saw: A Beginner's Guide — *John Burke*

MAGAZINES

WOODTURNING ◆ WOODCARVING

FURNITURE & CABINETMAKING

THE ROUTER ◆ WOODWORKING

THE DOLLS' HOUSE MAGAZINE

WATER GARDENING ◆ EXOTIC GARDENING

GARDEN CALENDAR

OUTDOOR PHOTOGRAPHY

BLACK & WHITE PHOTOGRAPHY

BUSINESSMATTERS

The above represents a full list of all titles currently published
or scheduled to be published.
All are available direct from the Publishers or through
bookshops, newsagents and specialist retailers.
To place an order, or to obtain a complete catalogue, contact:

**GMC Publications,
Castle Place, 166 High Street, Lewes,
East Sussex BN7 1XU, United Kingdom
Tel: 01273 488005 Fax: 01273 478606
E-mail: pubs@thegmcgroup.com**

Orders by credit card are accepted